THE BROKEN CISTERN

The
Broken Cistern

THE CLARK LECTURES 1952–53

by

BONAMY DOBRÉE

1955
INDIANA UNIVERSITY PRESS
Bloomington

PRINTED IN GREAT BRITAIN

PREFACE

THIS book contains the Clark Lectures 1952–53, and I would like first to express to the Master and Council of Trinity College, Cambridge, how sensible I am of the honour done me in inviting me to give the lectures, and to thank them for the many kindnesses shown me. Apart from a little necessary re-shuffling, I have in the main left as delivered these 'talks', I would prefer to call them, which were not designed for an audience of literary specialists, but, rather, as public lectures for such as cared to come.

The title of the series as given was 'Public Themes in English Poetry', for I hoped to show that if poetry is to be widely read, and retained in the minds of men, large commonly felt themes must provide a basis from which poets can explore other realms of experience. And then, as I thought about it all, it came to me to ponder why poetry to-day penetrates to the general reader less than its volume and quality would seem to deserve. May one of the reasons be, I asked myself, that so much of our current criticism, valuable in many ways, militates against the absorption of poetry by the public because it ignores that aspect? A verse adapted from Jeremiah (ii.13) seemed to me to describe the situation: 'They have forsaken . . . the fountain of living waters, and hewed them out cisterns, broken cisterns that can hold no water.' Whence my new title.

Some of my friends have told me that I am astray in hoping for poetry that is easier to understand than that usually offered us to-day, and that I am wishing for the wrong, the impossible thing. But we must distinguish between difficulties. No great poetry can be easy, though

v

some that is very-good indeed may be—Campion's, for example: but there is the difficulty of complex thought or feeling, and that of inspissated speech. Nobody, I think, would argue that 'La Belle Dame sans Merci' is an easy poem; but it is neither the language nor the imagery— I am not talking about symbolism—that offers any obstacle to understanding. I confess I fail to see why difficulty in itself is admirable, and I would maintain that nearly all great poetry has, on at least one level, something to give that the bulk of readers can receive at the first impact. And this something is very often a re-statement of some universal theme to which the great majority of human beings immediately respond.

It gives me great pleasure to have the opportunity to express the gratitude I feel for the help received from the staff in the Department of English Literature here while I was preparing these lectures. Mr A. J. Creedy offered me examples over the whole field, and also read the lectures and corrected errors; the late W. R. Childe and Mr Harold Fisch gave me great help where science was concerned, as did Dr A. C. Cawley of the English Language Department, while Mr Robin Skelton of the University of Manchester came to my aid in 'Stoicism'. My greatest debt is owing to Mr G. Wilson Knight, who, besides adding to my material in the lectures on science and Stoicism, by driving home the radical importance of Cranmer's speech in *Henry VIII* largely determined the whole pattern of my discourses on patriotism. Next, to my students, who after patiently listening to my early drafts, made some valuable criticisms which made me modify some personal idiosyncrasies. Finally, and not least, to my wife, whose insistence upon the need for clarity spurred me to such castigation of my prose as I had it in me to accomplish.

BONAMY DOBRÉE

The University, Leeds

October 1953

ACKNOWLEDGMENTS

My thanks are due to the authors, or their representatives, and the publishers concerned, for permission to include quotations from poems as under:

W. H. Auden	*Nones. Letters from Iceland. For the Time Being. New Country*	Messrs Faber & Faber
Francis Berry	*The Galloping Centaur*	Messrs Methuen & Co
Rupert Brooke	*Collected Poems*	Messrs Sidgwick & Jackson
Roy Campbell	*Talking Bronco*	Messrs Faber & Faber
Padraic Colum	'Nine'	The Author
Alex Comfort	*The Signal to Engage*	Messrs Routledge & Kegan Paul
C. Day Lewis	*Collected Poems 1929–1936*	Hogarth Press
Emily Dickinson	*Poems of Emily Dickinson*	Messrs Jonathan Cape
T. S. Eliot	*Collected Poems 1909–1935. Four Quartets*	Messrs Faber & Faber
Robert Graves	*No More Ghosts*	Messrs Arthur Barker
Ivor Gurney	*Severn and Somme*	Messrs Sidgwick & Jackson
Thomas Hardy	*The Dynasts. Collected Poems*	Trustees of the Hardy Estate, and Messrs Macmillan

J. Heath-Stubbs	Poem	The Author and Messrs Methuen
Hamish Henderson	*Elegies to the Dead in Cyrenaica*	Messrs John Lehmann
G. M. Hopkins	*Poems 1918*	Oxford University Press
A. E. Housman	*The Shropshire Lad*	Messrs Jonathan Cape
Rudyard Kipling	*Verse*, Definitive Edition 1940	Mrs George Bambridge and Messrs Methuen
James Kirkup	*A Correct Compassion*	The Author and Oxford University Press
Louis MacNeice	*Collected Poems 1925–1948*	Messrs Faber & Faber
Charles Madge	*New Country*	The Author
George Meredith	*Poems*	Messrs Constable
Robert Nichols	*Ardours and Endurances*	Messrs Chatto and Windus and Author's executors
Herbert Read	*Twenty-five Poems*	The Author
Alan Ross	*The Derelict Day*	Messrs John Lehmann
Edith Sitwell	*The Shadow of Cain*	The Author
Stephen Spender	*The Still Centre*	Messrs Faber & Faber
A. C. Swinburne	*Songs Before Sunrise*	Messrs Heinemann
Dylan Thomas	*Collected Poems*	Messrs J. M. Dent
John Wain	Poem	The Author
Gerald Walker	*Festival of Britain Prize Poems* (Penguin)	The Author
Rex Warner	*New Country*	The Author
Anthony Woodhouse	Poem	The Author
W. B. Yeats	*Collected Poems*	Mrs W. B. Yeats and Messrs Macmillan

CONTENTS

PUBLIC THEMES

AT the time I was invited to give these lectures, I had for a year or two, a little idly, been noting in my cursory reading how certain themes perpetually thread in and out of our poetry. Given a further motive, I pursued these with greater attention, not to follow the path of the history of ideas, but to see how the themes were variously treated by different poets. And as I went on I found that these themes came out most clearly in the poetry that is most read, most loved, and therefore most generally remembered. This led to my asking myself what, after all, is it that the great body of possible readers will receive, will recognise, will ask for even, by way of poetry? And so my pursuit, by an obvious step, brought me to a matter which is bound to given concern to anybody who cares for literature, namely the position of poetry to-day. It is notorious that it is, broadly speaking, little read, although a great deal is written. Besides what is published in book form, usually collected from journals, there are some fifty 'little magazines', mainly devoted to verse, scattered over the country. Yet we continually meet, in national papers of high repute, with such an assertion as 'literature is no longer the affair of educated people. Science, advertising and business offer more to the intelligence and imagination, not to say the pocket'. This, we hope, is an exaggeration: but it would certainly seem to be true that, as Mr Graham Hough has put it, poetry 'shows signs of becoming a sort of grumbling appendix—an organ of no obvious utility that seems to exist in order to cause intermittent twinges of distress'. We naturally ask for reasons.

I for one asked, is it that poets in the main no longer deal with broad portmanteau notions that men carry about with them as they go daily to and fro? Or is it—a common querulous moan—that poets have come to use language in a way so removed from ordinary talking that they seem to huddle in groups bandying the ideas and employing the idiom of a consoling freemasonry? Certainly the grand, sweeping colloquial manner of Ben Jonson, Dryden, Pope, Wordsworth, Browning has almost disappeared, though Mr Eliot has to some extent restored it. And then—a bodeful query for a man of my trade, that of a professor of English literature—is it that the activities we so zestfully, so devotedly pursue in universities, have by some suave irony turned back upon us? Do our labours, instead of knocking down barriers between poet and reader, succeed only in erecting Pyrenees?

No one, of course, will deny that our century has been tremendously fertile in original criticism, which has opened up fields of the utmost interest, and probed into obscure recesses. We have been urged to investigate the recondite significance of imagery and symbol, of paradox and ambiguity, of irony and wit, and to embark on the treacherous oceans of the philosophy of language. Poets have been 'integrated with' the ethos of their times, social and philosophical: moral yardsticks, congruous with or in opposition to the searchings of our own puzzled day, have been offered for our use. New instruments have been thrust into our hands, probes and scalpels, such as psycho-analysis, which enables us, we eagerly believe, to come closer than ever before to the being of authors. We claim to realise their meaning even better than they themselves did; for poets, we are told, often write other than they think, perhaps scarcely recognise what they are writing about—a doctrine of inspiration in which, if we miss Apollo, we encounter at least the minatory figures of Drs Jung and Freud. All these approaches, naturally, have their value, since every piece of knowledge serves to enlighten, every

fresh attack makes us more alert. There is no doubt that
the enjoyment and receptivity of those of us who continually study poetry have become enormously better organised, more subtle, and, I am bound to add, more stren-
uous than they used to be. But haven't we perhaps in our
efforts, praiseworthy if fruitless, to arrive at 'concrete stan-
dards of evaluation' too exclusively pursued some ultimate,
to the shouldering aside of what is most *commonly* valuable
in poetry?

For I ask myself in this series of questionings (which
you may think will never end), what is the general reader,
whom I pathetically believe still to exist, to make of all
these
          bewildering appliances
    For mastering the arts and sciences[1]

as that gay crusader, Mr W. H. Auden, put it? Haven't
these brisk gales of doctrine puffed away one vastly
important element, that of the ostensible themes of a
poetry which does not profitably lend itself to our way of
analysis, a poetry with deep-rooted *common* implications,
poetry that has come to be, as Ben Jonson said of Shakespeare's,
                         . . . distilled
    Through all the needful uses of our lives?

Not that I would for a moment deny that poetry is vital to
us in that it does actually open up new vistas of being—
the *un*common. All original art is an exploration of reality,
disturbing us, awakening us by flashes of unique apprehension. It is the product of the creative imagination
grasping and modifying the experience that we call reality.
Yet poetry is also the vehicle for communicating what
would seem to be the basic and permanent emotions
through which the mass of humanity lives out its life,
feelings shared at various levels, feelings moreover which
partly determine, and partly are the result of, what we
vaguely term 'an attitude to life'. As Dr Tillyard has reminded us:

Poetry is concerned with large general states of mind. . . .
Some of these states of mind recur so regularly through the ages
that they appear timeless and are always easy of apprehension.
The poet is bound to meet them and to want to give his version
of them. And the reader enjoys it because it makes what he
already knows live more intensely in his mind.[2]

Is this to any large degree true of the poet to-day? Does
he want to give his version of large general states of mind?
Very rarely, it would seem. Nevertheless certain groups of
feelings are obviously essential to humanity, or why should
they be so persistent? They are, inevitably, coloured by
circumstance; and, again, transformed by the poets, who
by their particular and usually deeper vision, reinforce,
modify, or bring to keener awareness their readers' own
intuitions.

Sometimes the poet's realisation has stirred him in such
a way that he can embody it only in difficult symbol; it
may come to him as such: but often he has made his statement in utterances which though perfectly plain and direct
are, all the same, memorable. We tend, however, to neg-
lect such poetry in our studies, as not being complex
enough; we scout its musical quality, forgetting that this
also—rhythm, vowel-sound, cadence—is itself symbol; we
incline to rate it low in the scale of imaginative vision, perhaps because we agree with Mr Edwin Muir that 'There
seems to be a rule by which, in our time, the more an
imaginative work of art contains, the less it communi-
cates', the implication being that a poem which at once
affects us cannot have much to reveal. So I am convinced
that it would be worth while to adopt a simpler approach,
releasing ourselves from the more demanding analytical
procedures, and ridding ourselves of the jargon which,
originally a convenient shorthand, lends itself to obfus-
cating dogma. And I would plead (at least with regard to
the themes I am tracking) that we should take it that the
poet knows, deep in his fibres, what he wishes to testify
to; and that when such a theme appears in his verse he has

willed it so; or, if obtruding uncalled for, has been content
to let it insist. For this poetry, concerned with great universal themes that touch everybody, and that all can
grasp, has a constant connection with the life of everyday
at its deeper, and therefore usually unexpressed, levels. If
then it illumines what goes on beneath the surface of our
daily being, I submit that it should be part of the normal
activity of criticism to dwell upon it.

Thinking as I did in this way, my discourses, beginning
as description of a search prompted by curiosity, became an
argument—if fumbling towards a conclusion can be
accounted as argument. The main body of my lectures
still consists of the tale of my journeyings; but then, finding, as I think I have done, that poetry does not fulfil its
great civilising function unless it is suffused with, or at
least supported by, some great accepted theme, I have
suggested that one of the reasons why poetry is not much
read to-day is that such themes are absent; and further,
that this absence may be due to the kind of criticism to
which poetry is subjected. I am still far, perhaps always
shall be far, from arriving at well-rounded conclusions,
though I shall risk some at the end of this book. So I would
ask you to look upon these discourses as my stumblings
along a path which others may travel with steps that are
more assured.

Three themes which presented themselves, among
others which anybody can think of, were Stoicism, Scientism—I am advisedly using the new-fangled term—and
Patriotism, which have emerged with varying pervasive-
ness in our poetry since the sixteenth century, though not
then for the first time. Because throughout these years they
crop up so unexpectedly, so incongruously even, often
through most unlikely agents,* I had orginally called

* Who, for instance, reading a poem beginning:
      What shall I do for the land that bred me?
with a varied chorus running:
      Under her banner I'll live [or die] for her honour
would immediately attribute it to Gerard Hopkins?

them 'underlying themes'. They carry more than a little part of the assumptions, conscious or not, by which (I believe) the great majority of people, whether they think or just jog along, act out their lives. They branch out from feelings lying deeper than the work-a-day mind, though not unreachable by common thought. They might be called the great impersonal themes. They seldom issue by themselves, separated from other emotive ideas, in such intense poetic form as do the personal ones, those of love, or revealed religion, and therefore don't suffer such close and lingering study as the latter. Yet they certainly rank as major themes, at all events when they come to affect man's vision of himself, thus liberating the imagination; but they haven't the fierce individuality that we find, say, in the love poetry of Donne or the 'terrible sonnets' of Hopkins. My themes, in short, have to do not so much with the isolated creature as with the human situation. Thus it seemed to me that the best title for them was 'public'.

It may be objected that the poetry carrying these themes is usually 'mere' poetry of statement (why, by the way, the damning adjective?); but I would reply that here also reality is being explored, a reality that matters, not simply to the individual poet, but to all of us as members of the human family. They haven't evoked precisely parallel poetic treatment, or called for the same form, since, corresponding as they do with diverse feelings, their poetries belong to rather different categories, which a De Quincey might label as those of power, knowledge, and sentiment, though the boundaries of these are fluid enough. However that may be, I propose as the major part of my study to make a first rough investigation, with a somewhat arbitrary choice of poets, into the way these 'attitudes' have at various times, from the late sixteenth century to the present day, compelled poets to utterance, that is, to exploration of being; into what, in short, the poets have made of these themes, how these have changed, and whether there is any general law of change. You might call it a natural history of themes, leading to a consideration of whether the appearance of these themes has any connection with the sort of poetry that will engage a large number of readers.

The 'law of nature' I am working on from my first observations is something of this kind. An idea, a sentiment, a curiosity, enters general consciousness. It appears in poetry to begin with as didactic verse, plain poetry, moving gradually to the descriptive, and finally becoming symbolic, and, while developing, carrying an ever heavier superstructure of allied intuitions. Once it has attained its greatest poetic expression it exhausts, at least temporarily, its potentialities; it is no longer subject to the modifying power of the imagination. Also, perhaps, it ceases to move the general reader as being too commonplace; only certain commonplaces can be redeemed, by great poets, from dullness. The theme therefore becomes submerged, or absorbed into other themes, or possibly enlarged into something beyond itself. There is, however, no fixed pattern, as will be seen from the tentative reviews that follow.

CHAPTER I

STOICISM I

My first theme is Stoicism—the Roman sort of Seneca, Marcus Aurelius, and Epictetus; and I hasten to say that though I shall often enough fall back upon classical writings, this is in no sense a trudge along the old worn path of classical influence. At the moment that is not the point. Besides, I use Stoicism as a wide inclusive term, admittedly vague. Popularly it means 'putting up with things'; it denotes, as the *New English Dictionary* records in the first place, 'austerity, repression of feeling, fortitude'. The Stoic is defined as 'one who practises repression of emotion, indifference to pleasure or pain, and patient endurance'. If it were only that it would not carry poetry very far. Yet this usually accepted meaning describes well enough an attitude common in the average human: it neighbours, you may say, animal endurance; yet it is worth noting that when a man bears up against disagreeables, or pain, or disaster, he is vulgarly said to 'take the matter philosophically'. I don't imagine that Stoicism of this kind is the peculiar possession of the English—even if we all live by it a good deal—though it points to something that our best-known slogan during the last war was not glorifying nor patriotic, as with some nations, but quite simply 'We can take it.' No doubt a whiff of Stoical pride enters there too—after all, a man must strut a little sometimes. How far this is part of our make-up may perhaps be gauged by the answer given by a distinguished Master of a Cambridge College when asked what it was in his view made our soldiers suffer so patiently the grim conditions of active warfare: 'Oh, Stoicism, I suppose.' This 'sticking it' as you might say, would hardly seem to offer what Emerson called 'a metre-making theme'; and, in fact, it has not been much touched upon by our poets, even by our war poets, though it sometimes comes out, as with Mr Alan Ross:

> I watch the troops
> emerge from their crowded and cramped quarters,
> cigarettes burning in mouths, their eyes staring
> out to sea, clumsily grappling after some equation,
> with nothing more to understand but merely
> the plain necessity that breaks into their lives,
> demanding courage, tact and a new acceptance.[3]

The dogged metre, the subdued tone with its occasional sharp tap, suggests only too well a tortoise-like state of being. The inclusion, however, of other, deeper elements of Stoicism, drawing on a wider vision, a more imaginative apprehension, produces different poetry. When Sir Herbert Read's soldier of the earlier war hails a conscript of 1940 he tells him:

> There are heroes who have heard the rally and have seen
> The glitter of the garland round their head. . . .

> Theirs is the hollow victory. They are deceived.
> But you, my brother and my ghost, if you can go
> Knowing that there is no reward, no certain use
> In all your sacrifice, then honour is reprieved.

> To fight without hope is to fight with grace,
> The self reconstructed, the false heart repaired.[4]

With the phrasing and diction perfectly in tune, with the occasional rhyme giving precision, this mirrors what is perhaps the ultimate moral Stoicism; not only endurance, the leaving aside of what is beyond the will, but the achievement of an integrity at once proud and humble, together with a free acceptance.

I would like to pause a moment on those two examples. The first is partly descriptive; the sentiment is one everybody is familiar with; it is very simple verse, almost the

poetry of statement. The second passage is of far higher
potential; it is tense with meaning; it contains imagery—
'the glitter of the garland'; the 'hollow victory'; the basic
sense is made to carry an enormous superstructure of ideas.
Perhaps the variety of treatment is significant of what happens with public themes.

Herbert Read gathers together some of the many elements of Stoicism which have moved English poets; beyond them there is the religious ethos in which they are
set. I use 'religious' in a large signification, the sense a
man may have of his being part of some mysterious process working itself out, a progress only 'perhaps' to some
far-off divine event, to which man must submit himself as
best he may, with as much understanding as he can arrive
at. And within this process he must willy-nilly maintain
himself as a free, self-governing unit of being:

> Will is as free as any emperour,
> Nought can restrain her *gentle* libertie;
> No tyrant, nor no torment, hath the power,
> To make vs *will*, when we vnwilling bee.[5]

The human will *is* valid, in spite of such determinism as
the religious apprehension of Stoicism may tangle us in.
This shares, obviously, much of the ethic common to all
religions, and to contemplative or mystic philosophies,
even to that body of intuitive wisdom we call 'the Peren-
nial Philosophy'. I am not, of course, concerned with how
far a member of a Church could accept Stoicism as a religion, since, apart from all questions of dogma or the necessity for ritual, it maintains that man can be, indeed must
be, sufficient unto himself. What is of real significance to
me in my quest is the frequency with which Stoic notions
appear, so often as to suggest that they are perpetually
underlying attitudes. They cohere so as to become one of
those 'general states of mind' which have a pervasive
meaning for us, not merely as amateurs of literature, but as
men and women engaged in divers affairs. Emotive ideas

which crop up so constantly in our poetry must be among
those by which we live: they are part of our awareness, an
item in our consciousness of life.

I shall treat Stoicism in the main chronologically, because of my three subjects it seems most simply to illustrate the natural history of the public theme. When it
first entered English poetry it would be rash to guess.
Chaucer was at least aware of it, perhaps through Boethius:
at all events it thrust its way in clearly, we might say tem-
pestuously, when, from the middle of the sixteenth century, Englishmen were drastically troubled in their minds.
As Mr T. S. Eliot says, 'Roman Stoicism was in its own
time a development in self-consciousness; taken up into
Christianity, it broke loose again in the dissolution of the
Renaissance.'⁶ Perhaps the very extent to which it had
been 'taken up', maybe through the reversion to St
Augustine at and after the Reformation, made the 'breaking
loose' all the more easy. Every Christian had been taught
that we are all members one of another, so all would feel
comfortably at home on reading in Marcus Aurelius that
'We are all made for mutual Assistance, no less than the
Parts of the Body are for the Service of the whole.' And
had not St Ambrose taught that the blessed life depended
upon the favourite Stoic virtue of *honestas*, which we might
translate 'decency'—love thy neighbour as thyself? Therefore much was already to hand for a Stoic vogue even before
the Protestant revolution challenged the old ecclesiastical
authority, and drove man more and more to be his own
arbiter, this again while the revolution in scientific thought
was causing confusion by a similar withdrawal of authority; the Baconian road of certainty had not yet been
opened. So at an ecclesiastically chaotic time, when man
lacked that infallible guide he seems always to hanker
after, the new philosophy also shook his sense of security.
Thus it became intensely important to man to know himself. He needed to look at himself afresh, to re-assess his
nature, and his place in the scheme of things. It would

seem that the pressure born of this profound need caused
Stoical thought, which had so far been a mere shy trickle,
to swell into a torrent which flooded Elizabethan and
Jacobean literature, seeping in even to theological thought.
Hooker subtilised it in such phrases as:

> ... that which men have at all times learned, Nature herself must
> needs have taught; and God being the author of Nature, her
> voice is but his instrument.

Bishop Hall made no bones about it. 'If only', he exclaimed
in his *Heaven Upon Earth, a Discourse on the True Peace
and Tranquillity of the Mind*, if only Seneca 'could have
had grace to his wit, what wonders he would have done in
this Land'.

Of course, the ideas of Stoicism did not present themselves as a system in the minds of most men, though they
seem to have done so sometimes in those of the poets.
Indeed the conclusion of the first section of Sir John
Davies's *Nosce Teipsum*, from which I have already quoted,
and which treats 'Of Humane Knowledge', might almost
have been designed as the Stoic's *vade mecum*. In well-
known stanzas—why, we may ask, *are* they well known if
not that we respond to them readily now?—he enshrines
two contradictory strands of Stoical thought, pride and
humility:

> I know my *Soule* hath power to know all things,
> Yet is she blinde and ignorant in all;
> I know I am one of Nature's little kings,
> Yet to the least and vilest things am thrall.

> I know my life's a paine and but a span,
> I know my *Sense* is mockt with euery thing:
> And to conclude, I know my selfe a MAN,
> Which is a *proud*, and yet a *wretched* thing.[5]

It would be difficult to maintain that that is great poetry,
though it stays in the mind; but what a response it must
have met with among those weltering in, say, Gascoigne's
Drum of Doomsday, in which man was assured, in the old

familiar way, that he was no more than a miserable ble-
mish, part of a 'continual mass of corruption which always
stinketh and is filthy and odious and horrible'! What
Elizabethan heart would not leap up to the appeal to
pride? But Davies, you feel, is clearing his ideas, imparting
them in plain straightforward words. In short, *Nosce Teipsum* is didactic poetry, the first phase in the treatment of a
theme. The pressure the ideas produced was not great
enough to make Davies seize truth intuitively rather than
intellectually. It had been otherwise in *Orchestra*, where
his vision of the dancing harmony of the whole universe
produced a poetic impulse which gave birth to an exu-
berant fantasy in beautifully controlled images. Yet if the
stanzas I quoted exhibit little imagery, which we have
come, too much perhaps, to regard as the hall-mark of
good poetry, there is an insistence in the rhythm which
gives the poem a certain urgency, a gravity in the vowel-
colouring which gives it depth.

Naturally, if a poet merely drapes philosophical ideas in
the clothing of verse—the old phrase is applicable here—
he is not imaginatively grasping reality at the level where
it is almost bound to present itself in symbols. It is only
when a 'philosophy' (I use the term loosely) so enters
into a man that it forms part of the nourishment by which
he lives, that his poetry can achieve the fusion of self and
idea which makes every good poem a unique thing. Then
it becomes an addition to our own sense of reality. For
'poetry *thinks*', as Mr R. P. Blackmur notes, 'by giving
the actual experience—the make-believe—of thought: it
does not convert thought into poetry except at the expense
of both.'[7] Thus for poetic pressure to be induced to the
extent where the ideas come to the poet in the form of
imagery, he must be unaware of the ideas as a system. They
are part of the earth he treads on. This seems almost to
have occurred with Samuel Daniel, especially in his
'Epistle to the Lady Margaret, Countess of Cumberland',
a poem Wordsworth found 'very beautiful', incorporating

a stanza of it in *The Excursion*. In a note he quoted four others, 'as they contain', he said, 'an admirable picture of a wise Man's mind in a time of public commotion'.[8] The poem is much more than that: it is the most glowing, the most intensely communicated direct expression of Stoicism in the language. The splendid assurance of the opening lines seems to celebrate a moral victory:

> He that of such a height hath built his mind,
> And rear'd the dwelling of his thought so strong,
> As neither fear nor hope can shake the frame
> Of his resolvéd pow'rs, nor all the wind
> Of vanity or malice pierce to wrong
> His settled peace, or to disturb the same;
> What a fair seat hath he, from whence he may
> The boundless wastes and wilds of man survey.

the next stanza developing the imagery of the castle built securely while wars surge around it.

What sort of thing have we got here? The sentiments can easily be paralleled in any Roman Stoic writings:[9] but as we read them there they make an impact on our minds alone, as rather smug moral apothegms. Daniel is doing something other. If he were not, how would the ordinary reader react to the injunction not only to be free of all hurt, but as he goes on to say, to regard 'honour, power, renown' as 'gay afflictions'? These do not as a rule figure in the pattern of his life. Daniel, we see, does two things. He stirs the imagination by his imagery, by the music, and by the beautifully ordered movement of the whole poem; then he universalises, making the idea available at levels everybody can experience, by virtually translating Seneca's ejaculation 'Oh, what a contemptible object a man is unless he can raise himself above being a man!'*

> Knowing the heart of man is set to be
> The centre of this world, about the which
> These revolutions of disturbances

* O quam contempta res est homo, nisi supra humanum se erexerit.

> Still roll; where all th'aspects of misery
> Predominate; whose strong effects are such
> As he must bear, being pow'rless to redress;
> And that unless above himself he can
> Erect himself, how poor a thing is man!

The whole treatment is a stage beyond that of *Nosce Teipsum*. It is no longer what we call didactic poetry, though teach it does. But then in a sense, all art is didactic. Here, however, we are beyond plain statement: something is added to it—and to the reader. And probably, given that content, no more could be done with the theme. The subjugation of the natural animal, and his elevation, had been expatiated upon; sublime indifference belauded. 'Admirable, no doubt!' the ordinary man might say, 'but why?'

Man needs the answer; and the theme, to live, had to be enriched, to be expanded. So far it satisfied the common Elizabethan desire to find, self-protectively, a stable balance amid the disturbed, swaying opinions of the time, a time moreover turbulent, violent, disrupted, full of wild imaginings, of threats of plague or torture. But how if it should become a brake upon vital instincts? What was lacking to make it a poetic public theme was what I have called the religious element in Stoicism, such as Chapman strove to urge upon the playgoers. Since it was new, probably, to the groundlings, its presentation was flatly didactic, of set purpose one would suppose from *The Revenge of Bussy d'Ambois*, for Chapman was a great poet who did not normally write in this way. It may be that through the speeches of Clermont he was defending Stoicism against the refutation of it in *Hamlet*, which among its wealth of themes contains a criticism of the Stoic attitude Chapman had rammed ruthlessly home in his earlier play *Bussy d'Ambois*. All very fine, Shakespeare seems to be saying. Horatio is a magnificent fellow; being

> As one in suffering all, that suffers nothing,
> A man that fortune's buffets and rewards

had ta'en with equal thanks. Because as a good Stoic he
was not passion's slave, Hamlet would wish to wear him
in his heart's core. Yet now we meet—significantly for my
thesis—one of the most quoted remarks in the whole
language: 'There are more things in Heaven and earth,
Horatio, than are dreamt of in your philosophy.' There
Hamlet was reflecting our curious duality of feeling towards Stoicism; we are strongly attracted, but we handle
it gingerly, stopping short of embracing it as a wholly
satisfying means to life. Clermont, the 'Senecal man', had
he been in Horatio's place, would have answered:

> That in this one thing, all the discipline
> Of manners and of manhood is contain'd:—
> A man to join himself with th'Universe
> In his main sway, and make (in all things fit)
> One with that All, and go on, round as it:
> Not plucking from the whole his wretched part,
> And into straits, or into nought revert,
> Wishing the complete Universe might be
> Subject to such a rag of it as he;
> But to consider great Necessity,
> All things refract as well as voluntary
> Reduceth to the prime celestial cause
> Which he that yields to with a man's applause,
> And cheek by cheek goes, crossing it no breath,
> But like God's image, follows to the death,
> That man is truly wise . . .[10]

It is obvious that to make Stoicism into a public dramatic
theme was engagingly easy. It ran counter to no world-
picture; it could very happily be fitted into any scheme of
Wheels of Fortune, Chains of Being, Cosmic Correspondences or almost anything. Chapman, very neatly, in an
age much given to Calvinism, emphasised determinism,
great Necessity. He wove popular ideas into the theme,
gave precision, and a new direction, to what people were
obscurely thinking. Some, however, might find such
Stoicism too capacious a sack, as does Mr Eliot in the

C

passage I have already quoted from. Referring to this very speech he goes on:

> A man does not join himself with the universe so long as he has anything else to join himself with; . . . Stoicism is the refuge of the individual in an indifferent or hostile world too big for him. . . . The Stoical attitude is the reverse of Christian humility.

Clermont might have answered that joining one's self with the universe is simply living according to nature, then a plausible doctrine. And that it has a humility of its own he had tried to express in the clause beginning 'Not plucking from the whole his wretched part': and he would no doubt have referred to Marcus Aurelius for support:

> He that frets himself *Sore* because Things don't happen just as he would have them, is but a sort of *Ulcer* of the World; by murmuring at the Course of Nature he quits the Universal Body, and gains only the distinction of a Disease.[11]

And he actually did say:

> He that strives t'invert
> The Universal's course with his poor way,
> Not only dust-like shivers with the sway,
> But, crossing God in his great work, all earth
> Bears not so cursed and so damn'd a birth.[12]

He would have called that humility: but humility, as many have discovered, is one of the most insidious forms of spiritual pride.

None of this, however, is my affair, which is to see how the general acceptance of Stoicism as a sense of life constituted it a public theme engendering the sort of poetic pressure that can issue in imaginative verse. So far the result had been chiefly didactic, directly so with Davies and Chapman, with Daniel made more subtle, more piercing, by figurative language.

We turn naturally to the theatre if we want to know what was going on in the general mind in Elizabethan times, for there poets have to deal with matters that are sure of an

immediate popular response. Stoicism was rampant on the
Elizabethan stage, and it would be interesting if we could
trace how far the purely literary irruption of Senecan
drama did actually affect our attitude to life, or whether
the early fashion for Senecan plays in some way set its mark
upon our national character. The attractive game had been
started by Jasper Heywood in Cambridge as early as
1559 with his *Troades*, and it was pursued with loud
halloes till well into the next century. I shall not go over
the course; this has been brilliantly done by many writers,
and is not really to my purpose. For the average playgoer,
we may be sure, did not care a fig for the faithfully Senecan constructions of Daniel or Sir William Alexander, if
he ever saw them; and Ben Jonson's more wayward treatment proved a failure. What he revelled in were the grue-
some scenes such as he found in Kyd and Tourneur; but
he also, one suspects, relished the 'moral sentences', much
as an audience to-day dotes upon the juicy wise-crack.
There is no need to comb the playwrights for these, they
offer themselves everywhere; and it is interesting, or amusing, to find Stoic sentiments, even when they are not *sen-
tentiae*, in plays which are in no obvious way Senecan
imitations, as when in *The White Divell* Antonelli says to
Lodovico 'Have a full man within you'. Playwrights could
confidently fall back on Stoic notions sure of the response
in the mass of their audience. They knew that they were
general ideas.

There may have been a touch of self-consciousness
about much of this; but with Shakespeare the attitude
is completely absorbed, as though he were unaware of
any doctrine, except, of course, in *Hamlet*. You can, it is
notorious, find anything you like to look for in Shakespeare, and I am not trying to make him out a Stoic. You
can, again if you like, relate many dramatic reactions in
his plays to a Stoic origin, since what I have called Stoicism embraces so much of what is general. Even for the
great scene in *Macbeth* when Macduff hears of the murder

of his wife and children, and Malcolm urges him to 'dispute it like a man', you can find in Seneca a parallel to Macduff's answer 'But I must also feel it as a man.'* Stoicism, after all, is not 'indifferent' in the vulgar sense, not unfeeling. If it were it would not have made the appeal it so evidently did, the appeal that Daniel makes to the Lady Margaret when he tells her that the man he is putting before her as perfectly wise,

> Cannot but pity the perplexed state
> Of troublous and distrest mortality:

but whereas with Daniel you still feel a little that he is clothing the idea with words, with Shakespeare the fusion is complete; the intuition and the words come simultaneously.

This is especially so in *King Lear*, a play admittedly interwoven with Stoical threads, many of them, it is very much to my purpose to note, vividly colouring the quotations which have become most popular: for example 'Bear free and patient thoughts'. There is again

> Men must endure
> Their going hence even as their coming hither:

life must be lived out: a Stoic commonplace. But then the transformation occurs, the raising of the whole theme to a brilliant imaginative level with 'Ripeness is all'. No sense of didacticism is left. Shakespeare is not telling us something; he is saying something.

'Ripeness is all' is one of those magic phrase that opens a hundred doors to the imagination. For one thing it includes in its reverberating overtones the Stoic idea of fullness, of being the man you are, a note so common in Shakespeare, involving not only the pride of, say, being

---

* Some accidents there are which I confess may affect [a man]; as Bodily Pains, loss of Children and Friends; the Ruin and Desolation of a Man's Country. One must be made of Stone or Iron, not to be sensible of these Calamities; and besides, it were no Virtue to *bear* them, if a Body did not *feel* them.—*Seneca's Morals*, trs. L'Estrange, p. 107.

Anthony still, but of being fully whatever you may happen
to be: even Parolles will live by being the thing he is.
The sense of this appears again and again in this period, as
in Marston's:

> Spite of despite, and rancor's villany,
> I am myself, so is my poesy.[13]

In the end, as men and women, we have always to live by
a sense of our own being, whatever the psychologists may
tell us to-day about the illusory nature of self; we all
imbibe this partly from our poets, who are maintainers of
tradition as well as innovators. As children, dabbling in
poetry we absorb all sorts of notions, the Stoical among
them, whitely innocent of where they come from. Who
among us, if he read poetry at all in adolescence, did not
come across and mutter over the lines in Ben Jonson's Ode
to Cary and Morison;

> It is not growing like a tree
> In bulk, doth make man better be;
> Or standing long an oak, three hundred year
> To fall a log at last, dry, bald and sere:
> A lily of a day
> Is fairer far in May
> Although it fall and die that night;
> It was the plant and flower of light.
> In small proportions we just beauties see;
> And in small measures life may perfect be.

Jonson, we know, was permeated by the classics; they
were part of his blood, and here at least they have become
part of ours by the force of the imagination making the
abstract actual. Seneca phrased this apprehension intellectually:

Life is long if it be full; but it is full when the mind has achieved
its development and realised its capacities. . . . ['Have a full man
within you': 'Ripeness is all'.] As a man of small stature may be
a perfect man; so in a small measure of time, life may be perfect.

Age is among the things external to us. How long I may live is an accident; but how long I may be a man, depends upon myself.[14]

With us, thanks to Ben Jonson, this notion has become intuitive.

If the function of poets is to make us, as common men, more vividly aware of the common apprehensions of being —I will not call them thoughts—or to universalise, how could they have avoided these stubborn sentiments, the most widespread, the most essential to decent living? They represent what we might call man's sense of his dignity by the mere fact of his being a man at all, the pride within humility without which he cannot live. In the speech of the common man these sentiments might run something like this: 'I am a mere speck of dust in the scheme of things. I suppose I must do my best to fit in. I'm pretty helpless against circumstance, but I know what the decent thing to do is. I may be an insignificant atom, but at least I have the sense of myself as a man, something that is a part of some no doubt divine process. I mustn't let it down.' All this would seem profoundly deep-seated in us, and evidently so general a state of mind is one to which poets are bound to respond. And what I am trying to follow is how the poets have brought this dull, underlying feeling, shared by everybody, within the realm of imaginative language, which makes a man possessor of his feelings, enlightens, and releases.

But just as there are moments when a man feels that the Stoic virtues may thwart a full realisation of life and like Leonato in *Much Ado* refuses to patch grief with proverbs, so there are times when so vague an 'attitude to life' cannot suffice for the general consciousness. One would imagine that men's temper during the fierce political quarrels of the early seventeenth century, embittered by metaphysical conflicts, would probably be inimical to it. All the same it now and again cropped up, as though it could even under those conditions produce pressure in the poetic

mind. Everybody is familiar with the last gloriously de-
fiant stanza of Lovelace's 'To Althea, from Prison'; Lovelace giving us also his enticing poem 'The Grasshopper',
where he impresses on the hapless insect that 'he that wants
himself is poor indeed'. The expression is sporadic, yet
before the clash gathered to its head in the Great Rebellion the theme came to splendid utterance in *Comus*. This
is not private poetry; as a masque it was intended for the
general reader, if at a high level. We do not know what
schooling the Elder Brother had, but he certainly pro-
pounded good sound Stoical common sense when he
calmed his junior with:

> Peace, brother, be not over-exquisite
> To cast the fashion of uncertain evils;
> For grant they be so, while they rest unknown,
> What need a man forestall his date of grief
> And run to meet what he would most avoid?

And later, when he reassured his brother, increasingly dis-
tressed about what might befall the Lady, he uttered un-
exceptionable Stoic doctrine:

> . . . against the threats
> Of malice or of sorcery, or that power
> Which erring men call Chance, this I hold firm,
> Vertue may be assail'd, but never hurt,
> Surpriz'd by unjust force, but not enthrall'd . . .

which brings us to the very core of the Stoic belief that
supported its morality:

> . . . if this fail
> The pillar'd firmament is rott'ness,
> And earth's base built on stubble.

The substance is the same as Chapman's; and here also the
expression is dramatic, framed for public utterance relying
on immediate response. But it is more than poetry of statement; there is present a passion, a fervour of the creative
imagination working from poetic tension, manifest by the

idea being expressed in imagery, by the sonority of 'the
pillar'd firmament is rott'ness' and by the vehement alli-
teration of 'And earth's base built on stubble'.

Comus himself, we know, fleers at the Stoic renuncia-
tion of life—not the true doctrine. He speaks with withering scorn of

> . . . those budge doctors of the *Stoick* Furr

(Milton's 'canine r' being reinforced by the double letter)

> Who fetch their precepts from the *Cynick* Tub
> Praising the lean and sallow abstinence.

True, the speech, where he describes life 'if all the world
Should in a fit of temperance feed on pulse' merely con-
forms, it may be said, to dramatic decorum. After all, if
you are going to invite a Lady to participate in all sen-
sual delights you will be anxious to make those who despise them as horrid as possible. Yet there is as well something of the young Milton in this speech, so splendid, so
glowing, so varied in imaging and in subtle rhythmic
movement. Being so much, as Dr Leavis has rightly
pointed out, the most Shakespearean passage that Milton
ever wrote, it makes us wonder whether here too Milton
was not of the Devil's party whether he knew it or no.

Indeed Milton was, in common with many English
poets, prey to that strange duality with respect to Stoicism
I have already noted. Where do we, his readers, stand, for
instance, when we read *Paradise Lost*? All of us, however
much we may go on quarrelling about Satan, to some
degree admire him, at any rate before he has lost all his
original brightness; but is it not exactly where he echoes
the Romans, as in his emphasis on 'the unconquerable
will, . . . and courage never to submit or yield'? But on
which side, really, is Stoicism? Does not Michael's adju-
ration to Adam smack of the same origin?

> Nor love thy life, nor hate; but what thou livst
> Live well, how long or short permit to Heav'n.

And in *Paradise Regain'd* the very violence of Milton's
rejection in seven concentrated scornful lines betrays, as
Dr Hanford argues, the strong lure it had for him. That
poem, even more than *Paradise Lost*, was aimed at audience fit though few; and in his later work it would seem as
though Milton was not so much taking up what there was
of Stoicism in the popular mind and giving it back
deepened and enriched, as Shakespeare had done, but,
rather, wrestling with it as a personal problem. Nor again
was Dryden, a little later, enough imbued by it to present
it as a public theme: he also felt that odd ambivalence, if
the magnificent exordium of *Religio Laici* is any evidence:

> Some few, whose Lamp shone brighter, have been led
> From Cause to Cause, to *Nature's* secret head;
> And found that *one first principle* must be;
> But *what*, or *who*, that UNIVERSAL HE;
> Whether some *Soul* incompassing this Ball,
> *Unmade, unmov'd; yet making, moving* All, . . .
> One thought *Content* the Good to be enjoyed:
> This, every little *Accident* destroyed:
> The *wiser Madmen* did for *Vertue* toyl,
> A Thorny, or at best a barren soil: . . .

A rejection of Stoicism, certainly; but also an admission of
its potency, by the very richness of tone and pungency of
phrase.

By the time we get to Dryden, Stoicism as a public
theme had reached an advanced stage. Catching up a common but confused sense of life, it had gone through various
phases—the didactic, the descriptive, and that where
imagery alone will serve. It had had offshoots, merging
with other feelings common to men at all times, tending to
what we might call the Epicurean (which in England often
strongly tinctures the Stoic), or those we group under the
heading of Horatian retirement. There had been minor
poems, still (at least till quite recently) popular, such as
Wotton's 'Happy the man whose wish and care, A few
paternal acres bound'; that admirable lyricist Campion had

sung Stoical *honestas* in 'The Man of Life Upright'; Dyer
had given 'My mind to me a kingdom is', though perhaps
this last has about it a tang of that self-gratulation, com-
placency, or even priggish self-righteousness that revolted
Milton, into which Stoicism may too readily slip if unaccom-
panied by a sense of either humility or the stupendous
nature of the universal process. All this might be called
the plebeian acceptance of the doctrine, as opposed to the
aristocratic, which carries with it no easy comforts. At all
events the theme seems at this stage to have been complete
in itself; in the form it had reached it had no more to offer
the general reader by way of illumination, nor, if we are to
judge by Milton and Dryden, by way of assurance. And
here I might once more stress how ambiguous our attitude
towards Stoicism is. We live by it as an underlying statement of our position, but the moment we mention it by
name we reject it as not wholly satisfying. Take to-day, as
one example, Professor Day Lewis. In a very complex
poem he has the lines

> But look within my heart, see there
> The tough Stoic ghost of a pride was too severe
> To risk an armistice
> With lesser powers than death; but rather died
> Welcoming the iron in the soul
> Which keeps the spirit whole,
> Since none but ghosts are satisfied
> To see a glory passing and let it pass.[13]

That ambiguity has been constant; and if from the seventeenth century onwards Stoicism was to survive in poetry
as a public theme—and one would think that so persistent
an attitude to life would demand that it should—it would
need either some new stimulus to move the poets, or,
through them, some cross-fertilisation, or some sublima-
tion. Both of these, during the next few generations, sustained its poetic development, and kept it relevant to
living.

CHAPTER II

STOICISM II

I WOULD remind you that what I am concerned with in pursuing the natural history of public themes is the crystallisation in the imaginative vision of poets of common 'attitudes to life'. I have no wish to become involved in the history of ideas. Yet I must permit myself to turn aside for a moment to glance at the muddle of opinion prevalent in the early years of the eighteenth century; for at that time literature rubbed uncommonly familiar shoulders with the bustling life of everyday. Politics battled in verse, which sometimes became poetry, written even by Professors of Poetry. Victories were celebrated by reputable writers in more than one *Campaign*. The poets, who are so often fiercely opposed to, or in advance of, their age, since it is part of their function, then, with abnormal fidelity echoed the 'common sense' of the averagely thinking member of society. And in this period, ineptly labelled 'the age of reason', men were busily engaged in trying to find out how far reason was valid; and for the rest they enjoyed a terrific pother of clashing emotive ideas. The ordinary reader was assailed by a battery of notions attaching to the names of Spinoza, Descartes, Hobbes, Newton, Leibnitz, Locke, which caused a disturbance the scope of which most of us lazily leave unimagined. Since the fundamentals of Christianity seemed to be undermined more subtly than before, freethinkers, so-called and self-styled, flourished abundantly, and those who wrote, unafraid of honest vituperation, vociferously bandied about a wide variety of engaging heresies.

Amid all this tumult, Stoic literature throve. In 1693 Roger L'Estrange published a new translation of Seneca's *Moral Epistles*, which rushed on from edition to edition, reaching the tenth in 1711. In 1702, Jeremy Collier put out his much-thumbed Marcus Aurelius; and it has been estimated that during the century there were no fewer than fifty-eight issues of the *Meditations*. Everybody was permeated with Stoicism, even occasionally farm workers. At least Stephen Duck, the thresher poet, together with his fellow farm-hand, revered, so Spence tells us,[1] the name of L'Estrange because of his Senecan labours, though Duck found his chief delight in Epictetus. And how should there not be a vogue? The religious turmoils of the previous century, bloody, punitive, and unresolved, made men long for a doctrine of being which promised more quiet than the tedious clamours of which they were healthily fatigued. And here was Stoicism, which did not directly clash with Christianity, and held no conflicting dogmas men could imprison or kill each other about. How splendid! how delightful! how restful! Let us simplify, they seem to have said, and allow to drift away the smoke caused by the terrific explosion of ideas, metaphysical, scientific, political, economic, which had so alarmingly rocked the preceding generations. Moreover Stoicism,with its happy freedom from what Swift called 'the incohaerent jargon of the Schools', as well as from the rusted chains of Aristotelian physics, seemed to offer an air in which the average—and non-mathematical—man could breathe.

But here the poets, though willing enough to think like everybody else, fought a little shy. For the ordinary person Hobbism—though it was no longer socially decorous to admit agreeing with him—and the determinist side of Stoicism, played nicely into each other's hands. But the the very patness of it all made the poets a little uneasy. They had never glowed to the idea of imagination as fading memory, and had no liking for being securely manacled.* Or there was Locke's mechanistic universe—for whatever private reservations Locke may have had, to the common reader his universe was patently clockwork; and this at first sight seemed to buttress Stoic doctrine rather than revealed religion. Here was a sublime process going on to which man must submit. But to the poetic mind, at first over-nourished by the marvellously ordered working of Nature that Newton had illumined, the essentially un-creative character of the scheme in due course became repellent. Whether they knew it or not, they clubbed together with Shaftesbury—himself a frequenter of the Stoics, flexibly adapting much of their thought in his own vision—and cheerfully subjected the great body of the old doctrines to a blood transfusion. A number of them reani-mated it to the kind of excited Deism that sustains Thom-son's *Seasons*, and a good many other poems of the time.

If, however, we want to know, to feel even, the kind of mental-moral atmosphere in which men of that time lived, we turn to Pope, especially to the *Essay on Man*. In that staggering performance Pope triumphantly brought to the pitch of poetry nearly every thread of opinion-feeling cur-rent in his day. Some with De Quincey may regard it as a mere rag-bag of outworn notions; but in actual fact it is a consummate, brilliantly ordered digest of the underlying assumptions by which Pope and the men of his day largely lived. He did not dote on systems, any more than Swift, Shaftesbury, Berkeley or Bolingbroke:

> As drives the storm, at every door I knock,
> And house with Montagne now, and now with Lock,

and, obviously, with a good many others. That to the philosopher by trade the poem should seem an 'incohe-rent conglomeration of inconsistent theories', as Leslie Stephen found it to be, itself testifies to its reality as life: all of us, at any time, live by a set of assumptions that do not logically hang together. We are not, thank Heaven!

* Perhaps it was because Dryden had been alive to the implications of Hobbism that he had rejected Stoicism.

merely creatures of logic. Pope, while conceiving himself
a good son of the Church, fused with his Catholicism a
whole medley of concepts—the Great Chain of Being,
Progressivism tempered by a touch of Mandevillian down-
to-earth realism, Shaftesburian optimism offset by some of
the pessimism of the Christian humanist; in fact, everything, or almost. He solved, to his own satisfaction, the
problem of evil—a constant irritant to the men of his day
—by ramming home the point Dryden and Shaftesbury
had made, that our limited vision prevents us from seeing
the whole perfect design. Stoicism fitted in beautifully with
all this; but to claim, as had been done, that the *Essay* is a
poetic formulation of Stoicism is to overstate the case. In
one place at least Pope might be said to repudiate it by
declaring that man has 'too much weakness for the Stoic's
pride'. But then, again, since the whole poem aims at
deflating pride, this might suggest that were we made of
stouter stuff we might rise to Stoic heights. You can see
that he is fascinated, but at the same time repelled. Like
Milton and Dryden he is warily on guard against the lure.
For instance, in throwing out the phrases:

> In lazy Apathy let Stoics boast
> Their Virtue fix'd; 'tis fix'd as in a frost.[2]

he seems to be working up a scorn for the touch of chill
that breathes from Roman virtue. There was nothing pom-
pously complacent about Pope. But if he found the philosophy too rigid, too 'budge', as Comus has it, the essay
rings with echoes, and even more, of Seneca and the others.
He appears to be laying one set of ideas alongside another
to see if they really will cross-fertilise. Thus many of his
well-sounding dicta are queerly incomprehensible, absurd
even, unless we see where he got them from, what he was
trying to do.

For example, on the moral level, in the section he de-
votes to man's happiness, he lays down, without a tremor
it would seem, a maxim which makes us gasp:

> Take Nature's path, and mad Opinions leave;
> All states can reach it, and all heads conceive;
> Obvious her goods, in no extreme they dwell;
> There needs but thinking right, and meaning well.[3]

Rien que cela? we ask stupent. Is it really so simple, so easy after all, to think right and mean well? Yet the extravagant statement might not have seemed at all odd to Stephen Duck, who had no doubt read in his beloved L'Estrange:

> . . . This Consummated state of Felicity is only a submission to the Dictate of Right Nature: *the Foundation of it is Wisdom and Virtue*; the Knowledge of what we ought to do, and Conformity of the Will to that Knowledge.[4]

Pope, in fact, in striving to disentangle the problem of man's place in the universe, and how he ought to behave, was in the toils of Stoicism. He knew it, but he pretended innocence. Writing to Caryll, to whom he always played the orthodox good boy, he referred to, but discreetly did not quote, the grandly swinging:

> All are but parts of one stupendous whole,
> Whose body Nature is, and God the Soul,

which, he confessed uneasily, 'at the first glance may be taken for heathenism'. It may indeed! When in 1758 Elizabeth Carter wrote the Introduction to her translation of Epictetus, she remarked that the Stoics 'plainly speak of the World as God; or of God as the Soul of the World, which they call his substance'. In the passage I have snipped a couplet from, Pope was carrying the doctrine above the moral level to the religious, as he was, if not to quite so complete an extent, when he told his reader:

> All Nature is but art unknown to thee,
> All chance direction, which thou canst not see,[5]

which may be a happy filching from Shaftesbury, but derives anciently from Marcus Aurelius:

Providence shines clearly through the Administration of the
World: Even Chance itself is not without Steadiness and Nature
at the bottom; being only an effect of that Chain of Causes which
are under Providential regulation.[6]

Again, at the level of action, Pope's Stoicism is betrayed
by the flat statement

For know SELF-LOVE and SOCIAL are the same

which Professor Tawney, in his brilliant *Religion and the
Rise of Capitalism*, points to as evidence that in the early
eighteenth century capitalism had already found the slogan which made it free of the joyous realm of *laissez faire*.
But Pope may very well have been echoing Butler's *Ser-
mons*, and at any rate hated the moneyed interest, the
'silent growth of ten per cent' while 'in dirt and darkness
hundreds stink content'. It seems, however, simple to
suppose that he had culled from the *Meditations*:

Be you governed by the Reason within you; pursue that which
is most for your own and the Common Interest. For to speak
strictly, these Two are but one and the same.[7]

There is no need to labour the point. What we want to
see is what was happening to Stoicism as a public theme.
Pope himself was moulding it to cohere with his sense that
nature was continually creative, and that the poetic imagination was plastic, to use the jargon of the day. Whether
or not the *Essay* was contrary to Christianity, for him, at all
events, the universe was governed by, in his own phrase, a
'great Directing Mind', which pervades, fills, bounds and
equals all. It is manifest that Stoicism was no merely intellectual notion with him; something in it catalysed his
imagination. But in speaking for men, as a man and not as
a prophet, he summed up and gave a point to the underlying assumptions of his day. And not altogether by direct
statement. There is no rasping flavour of didacticism about
the *Essay*, if didacticism is, as Browning tells us, when a
poet takes up the harp 'only to speak dry words across its

strings'. He put Stoicism side by side with other matters that moved him, and his words were far from dry: the ideas produced enough poetic pressure in him to engender poetry. Statements of the old assumptions as found in L'Estrange or Collier would produce contemplative responses in those who conned them: as presented by Pope they modified common half-conscious assumptions, and sharpened the reactions in the mind of the general reader.

Yet though this was certainly a public theme—the poem was widely popular—this cross-fertilisation failed. The theme ceased to grow. The ageing century, perhaps, hardly needed that philosophy, since it had grown relatively stable, and was no longer seeking for ballast. We might expect something of the theme in Johnson, or possibly Cowper as he struggled for reassurance: but Collins, the Wartons, Gray were, with their age, one relieved from basic fears, curious to enhance the more fiery emotions, to explore the wild, or to experience, in the mediaeval revival, the strange. Certainly neither Smart's rapture nor Blake's visionary illuminations could find their account in it. And besides, notions can be taken too much for granted. Men get too used to them, and respond frostily. It becomes deadly dull to hear the same old things over and over again. Readers of the time, fed by the writings of the Stoics, or at least tasting them, did not want the accustomed food served up to them like a daily ration on a scarcely warmed platter of verse. For a thematic idea cannot, it seems, be just cross-fertilised; it needs to be sublimated if it is to remain vital. Either something new has to be added, or it has to be borne up on the wave of some other deep feeling, or some newly sensed assumption which can become a basis for living.

It fell to Wordsworth to re-infuse life into the theme. In his day men were once again feeling their foundations threatened; and in his work, especially the earlier, we cannot help being aware of Stoicism as a buoyant *underlying* theme. Underlying, because Wordsworth seems to have

D

been sustained by it without knowing it. He doesn't appear to have recognised its presence when he praised Daniel's Epistle 'To the Lady Margaret', and it was not for some thirty years after he had written the 'Ode to Duty' that he headed it, at the suggestion of Barron Field, with a relevant, if not unduly clarifying snippet, from Seneca's *Moral Epistles*. Professor Highet goes so far as to say that 'None has summed up the Stoic philosophy better than Wordsworth',[8] especially in his identification of duty with the deepest laws of physical nature. For him the lines

> Thou dost preserve the stars from wrong
> And the most ancient heavens, through Thee, are fresh and strong,

are incomprehensible if separated from the whole Stoical background of the poem.

But apart from that—and this is basic to my thesis— surely it is striking that the passages I shall quote from Wordsworth to support my contention turn out to be those that everybody knows, poems, or lines from poems, to which even those who are not professed Wordsworthians deeply respond. It was as though in voicing this particular attitude to life he was profoundly stirring in his readers sentiments so fundamental as to be normally subconscious, and, from the evidence, in widest commonalty spread. But Wordsworth enriched it all, carrying immeasurably further the process begun in the early eighteenth century of marrying it to a more modern sense of living. In the 'Ode to Duty' itself, Wordsworth does not rely upon, or evoke, merely what might be called the grimmer aspects of the old moral philosophy. We do not adhere to duty simply because there is nothing better we can think of to do. Duty is transmuted by, given warmth and intuitive meaning by, love as a unifying, a universalising power. All through Wordsworth we find this exalting, this re-creation indeed, of the old doctrine, achieved by formative language issuing under poetic pressure—the 'overflow of powerful emotions'. A rather clumsy early instance appears in *The Excursion*. There is a passage in Epictetus—it does not matter whether Wordsworth had read it or not—which runs:

> If God had created colours, and, in general, all visible things, but had not created a faculty to behold them, of what use would they be? None at all. If on the other hand He had created this faculty, but had not created objects of such a nature as to fal l under the faculty of vision, even so, of what use would it be? None at all.[9]

In the Preface to *The Excursion*—a passage which again 'everybody' knows, this is transformed, given immense voltage:

> How exquisitely the individual mind
> (And the progressive powers perhaps no less
> Of the whole species) to the external World
> Is fitted;—and how exquisitely, too—
> Theme this but little heard of among men—
> The external World is fitted to the Mind . . .

It would be foolish to object that actually the theme had often been heard in earlier days, embroidered not by Pope and Thomson alone, but by a score of poetasters; there, however, the application had been much more directly physical; not the individual mind, but, say, the individual nose. Certainly the thought with Epictetus is still more awkwardly embryonic than with these poets, and Wordsworth catches the theme up to an altogether higher level when, in referring to 'the progressive powers . . . of the whole species', he invokes the creative faculty of the mind. He is immensely transcending Epictetus when he requires that 'the discerning intellect of man' should be

> . . . wedded to this goodly universe
> In love and holy passion,

and should not merely accept it as something to be endured. Always in the passages which it does not seem

outrageous to call Stoical, there is conveyed a sense of
something far more *deeply* interfused than Professor
Highet's phrase 'summing-up' would cover. Wordsworth is not stating the ideas, he is living them; and
thus, through his poetry, we live them too. Yet anyone
taking up 'The Character of a Happy Warrior' fresh from
a reading of the *Discourses* might say, 'Why; this is sheer
Epictetus!' The lines about the happy warrior as one

> Whom neither shape nor danger can dismay,
> Nor thought of tender happiness betray

(a touch of Stoic rigour there!) will take such a reader
back to:

> Who then is the man who is invincible? He whom nothing
> beyond his will can dismay. So I go on observing him in each
> set of circumstances as if he were an athlete.[10]

In fact, nearly every line of the poem can be glossed from
the *Discourses*.

But in Wordsworth there is a sense of triumph, born
of continuous positive creative labour, no more than
latent, a modern reader would think, in Epictetus. We do
not feel that the latter's athlete, when called upon to face
some awful moment, will be happy as a lover, or attired
with sudden brightness. Nevertheless it is more than ever
plain, or so it seems to me, that much of the poetry that
we re-read and quote, and that gets itself by heart (who
doesn't carry 'The Happy Warrior' about in his mind's
pocket?) bears with it some sense of Stoicism, not as a
philosophy borrowed and flung over the shoulders like a
mackintosh, certainly not as a piece of classical adorn-
ment, but as a pervasive sense of being.

In Wordsworth, everybody knows, there is to be found
a great deal of matter which we associate rather with the
poets of the early eighteenth century than with the Romantic Revival; for example, what might roughly be called
Deism; but what for the Augustans was a kind of enve-

lope to contain a number of other impulses, for Wordsworth became a centralising mysticism. As far as what we
crudely call 'prose meaning' goes, there is little to choose
between the opening of the Hymn at the end of Thomson's
Seasons and Wordsworth's 'Influence of Natural Objects'.
Again, we might take

> Wisdom and Spirit of the Universe!
> Thou Soul that art the Eternity of Thought!

to be only a more powerful declaring the 'great Directing
Mind' that Pope postulated. The same basic apprehension is expressed, still more potently, in 'Lines Composed
above Tintern Abbey'; but this poem profoundly, with
miraculous shaft-like directness, transforms into poetry
the Stoic idea that man is a part of the physical world,
which is itself an expression of the god-head. Is there
any great difference, once more as far as prose meaning
goes, between the passage I shall quote in a moment—
superfluously, perhaps, since it is tucked away in everybody's memory, and this from Marcus Aurelius:

> All things intertwine with one another, in a holy bond:
> scarce one thing is disconnected from another. In due co-ordi-
> nation they combine from one and the same order. For the world-
> order is made out of all things, and God is one pervading all, and
> being is one, and law is one, even the common reason of all being
> possessed of mind . . . is one.[11]

That was from the *Cogitations*, and this is from *Tintern
Abbey*:

> I have felt
> A presence that disturbs me with the joy
> Of elevated thoughts; a sense sublime
> Of something far more deeply interfused,
> Whose dwelling is the light of setting suns,
> And the round ocean and the living air,
> And the blue sky, and in the mind of man:
> A motion and a spirit, that impels
> All thinking things, all objects of all thought,
> And rolls through all things.

There the old theme, dimmed by use, has become incandescent: Wordsworth has added another dimension. We get the electrically charged meaning that flashes out when thought and emotion are one, and present themselves, to the thinking, feeling mind, in imagery. The whole being acknowledges illumination. Whereas with Thomson we feel that he is fitting a dimly apprehended sense into a framework intellectually grasped, with Wordsworth it is a vision attempted, dared and won, realised perhaps only in the poetry itself. It is not a philosophic statement, but a 'presence': not as with Thomson a recognition of 'the varied god', but a 'sense sublime'.

It is something besides; and here I come back more directly to my thesis. Why is it that Wordsworth is so much part of us as a people? It is not because of the Romantic Revival, whatever that may have come to mean for most of us. All that is past history, it is none of our affair, and is even a little suspect. Because of his nature-description? We have always had that, and it goes on; we are even in danger of suffering from a surfeit of it. Perhaps it is something like this. Most of us have a shrub in our back garden; the roots are that set of assumptions I have called Stoicism. With many it hardly comes up at all, with others it produces a rather stiff arid shrub—the kind of thing Sir John Davies cultivated; or it may become well-branched and leafy, as with Daniel. With Wordsworth it became a magnificent flowering tree—from roots the same as ours. To put it differently, his intuition of existence, made available to us in his poetry, not only reflects, but clarifies, universalises, makes actual, what we all obscurely feel. The passages in his poetry which do this have become part of our national consciousness. The theme is a public one. Plenty of men confess that, lacking religious faith, they turn to Wordsworth; and Matthew Arnold's prophecy that poetry would take the place of religion has in their case come true. Moreover, it is largely because for Wordsworth this underlying sense, this Stoicism, was a thing he lived by, that it has become so for us in turn.

It took some time to be established at that level; these things always do take time. Even the later Romantics do not yield much to the casual tracker of themes. Not that one would expect to find much Stoicism in the full ardour of the movement, which, after all, in its vague recognised meaning, was precisely in rebellion against a good deal of what Stoicism stands for; its acceptance, its too rigid restriction of self, its particular sense of order and destiny. Romanticism exalted man, or at any rate his spirit, in a way from which the old Stoic would have recoiled as lacking in humility. It glorified passion and sensation; 'the feel of not to feel it' was to its poets the abomination of desolation, and certainly never to be told in rhyme. Byron is too dynamic to be Stoical, Shelley too self-willed; they have passionate worshippers, but are not taken to the hearts of the great body of general readers. Keats certainly achieved acceptance, but his is the acceptance, the ability to master perturbation, of the great artist. It has nothing to do with the *apatheia* of the Stoics, the resolute tranquillity which it was not fair of Pope to refer to as 'apathy', since in his day already the word was being used in our modern sense of lumpish indifference. The Stoical apathy is really just sound common sense; things happen because they are bound to happen; any event is the consequence of previous events; the wise man is unperturbed by results which he cannot help. A good topic, as we know, for a sermon by Bishop Butler, but not perhaps metre-making. In actuality, this sense can become poetic if intensely enough felt. Though arising from a vastly different source, for the common man it becomes much the same thing as Mr Eliot's 'Teach us to care and not to care, Teach us to sit still.'[12]

This sense is enormously wide-spread; it is related to the non-attachment sung in the *Bhagavad Gita*; but as A. C. Bradley said, 'The content of an idea is precisely the same whatever its origin may be.' So Stoicism of this

kind reveals itself even in Byron and Shelley, with both,
incongruously enough we might think, in association with
Prometheus—who refuses to accept. For Byron, Prometheus could 'strengthen Man with his own mind'; and
later we read:

> And Man in portions can foresee
> His own funereal destiny;
> His wretchedness and his resistance,
> And his sad unallied existence:
> To which his Spirit may oppose
> Itself—and equal to all woes,
>   And a firm will, and a deep sense,
> Which even in torture can descry
>   Its own concenter'd recompense,
> Triumphant where it does defy,
> And making Death a Victory.

There some alien elements creep in. From Shelley we have
the splendid utterance of Demogorgon at the end of *Prometheus Unbound*:

> Gentleness, Virtue, Wisdom and Endurance,
> These are the seals of that most firm assurance
>   Which bars the pit over destruction's strength . . .
> To suffer woes which hope thinks infinite;
> To forgive wrongs, darker than death or night,
>   To defy power which seems omnipotent;
> To love and bear; to hope till Hope creates
> From its own wreck the thing it contemplates . . .
> This is alone Life, Joy, Empire, and Victory.

A little too ecstatic, perhaps, for the true Stoic; but Shelley
again metamorphoses the doctrine, as happens when the
imaginative power transcends a philosophy or routine religion: and here we have Shelley formulating what he believed to be the highest man can attempt. His man, however, is not like Chapman's, subject to the main sway of the
universe, but out of its raw materials creates what he
desires, knowing it to be good. It is a vision of man reject-

ting the Stoic limitations, though achieving its rejection through an acceptance of its virtues. If this sort of Stoicism were the refuge of the individual in an indifferent or hostile world too big for him, as Mr Eliot affirms, it could certainly not produce poetry of this kind. In any case most religions provide this refuge for the mass of their votaries, certainly the Christian does, as cursory reference to any hymnal will show: then, however, it produces only minor, if often moving verse.

The theme seems to have attained its highest coherent development with Wordsworth, for with Shelley we already hear the first faint premonitions of its decline: it is being split up. We do not find it much, if at all in Shelley's successors, in many ways his heirs. Stoicism does not seem to have been their tacit basis of existence, nor that of the millions of readers of that prime favourite, *Festus*, where Bailey, as did his fellow Spasmodics, dealt, as he proudly said, with 'streams of feeling, passion's cataracts'. He bravely announced that

> We live in deeds, not years,
> In feelings, not in figures on a dial;
> We should count time by heart-throbs.

Hardly Stoical! It is not surprising that *Festus*, after being blown up to an incredible size, one day suddenly burst, and was hardly heard of any more. For after all, Stoicism of a kind—its self-control, its repression of feeling, its doctrine of belonging, of devotion to something other than self, its *honestas*, decency—was the recognised basis of Public School morality. *Festus* did not chime with that. And since at that time public school men provided the main body of readers, *Festus* went, and Stoicism continued as a public theme throughout the Victorian era, though sporadically, dwindling, broken up into its component parts.

There are echoes in Tennyson. Pallas in *Œnone* declares —again a well-known passage—

Self-reverence, self-knowledge, self-control,
These three alone lead life to sovereign power.
Yet not for power (power of herself
Would come uncalled for) but to live by law,
Acting the law we live by, without fear:
And because right is right, to follow right
Were wisdom in the scorn of consequence.

It has lost the intuitive spirit it had with Wordsworth; it
begins once more to smack a little of didacticism. Wisdom
has replaced love. The words, however, are not flat; there
is rhythm and music, even if there is no imagery. But
they give only a part of Stoicism; the pride in will is no
longer there. This last, however, was vehemently expressed by Swinburne, exulting in the primacy of man. The
poetic pressure induced by the idea bursts out in typically
Swinburnian exuberance:

Because man's soul is man's God still,
What wind soever waft his will
    Across the waves of day and night
    To port or shipwreck, left or right,
By shore and shoals of good and ill;
    And still its flame at mainmast height
Through the rent air that foam-flakes fill
    Sustains the indomitable light
Whence only man hath strength to steer
Or helm to handle without fear.

Save his own soul's light overhead,
None leads him, and none ever led,
    Across birth's hidden harbour-bar,
    Past youth where shoreward shallows are,
Through age that drives on through the red
    Vast void of sunset hailed from far,
To the equal waters of the dead;
    Save his own soul he hath no star.
And sinks, except his own soul guide,
Helmless in middle turn of tide.[13]

The Spasmodics, to be sure, might have approved the
fervour there; but in the sustained imagery, the controlled

pulsation of the rhythm, something other than excitement
emerges, not only the rejoicing in, but the steady acceptance of, man's responsibility for himself. It is not the
defiance blurted out by Henley (when he noisily declared
that he was master of his fate and captain of his soul) whose
outcries seem to voice a personal emotion rather than a
view of the human situation. One might well suppose that
in so individualistic an age as the Victorian, with its fierce
intellectual conflicts, its sense of progress, its evangelical
enthusiasms and its personal strivings, the Stoic lure would
be feeble. But even in poetry engendered by a personal
state of being, the general note may pierce through; and it
is not without significance for my thesis that it is Emily
Brontë who gives us, in 'The Old Stoic', the most poignant version in the age, all the more so because we connect it with her own life and the moving endurance of her
end:

> . . . if I pray, the only prayer
>   That moves my lips for me
> Is 'Leave the heart that now I bear
>   And give me liberty!'
>
> Yes, as my swift days near their goal,
>   'Tis all that I implore;
> In life and death a chainless soul
>   With courage to endure.

Again it is only part of the theme, and we are back at the
moral aspect. Indeed, it is noticeable that at this period the
religious vein in Stoicism is declining. It could not stall
together with the idea of evolution. Tennyson, we have
seen, suggests it vaguely in Œnone; but in Ulysses the
stress lies on the moral virtues that grace Telemachus and
make him a fit guardian of the home:

> Most blameless is he, centred in the sphere
> Of common duties, decent not to fail
> In offices of tenderness.

Telemachus is, in fact, a man Epictetus would have
approved of, 'one who considering the duties of life pre-

serves the natural and acquired relations; as a pious Person, as a Son, as a Brother, as a Father, as a Citizen'. Yet Ulysses himself has a vestige of the old Elizabethan Stoic pride, of being the thing he is:

> We are not now that strength which in old days
> Moved earth and heaven; that which we are we are.

The theme, however, is disintegrating, uncertain even in the one man of this time in whose poetry we might expect to find Stoicism, the lover of Marcus Aurelius, Matthew Arnold. With him it is wavering; he expresses it timidly when he verges on it, is sometimes hostile when he takes note of it. In 'The Gipsy Child by the Sea Shore' we come upon:

> Is the calm thine of Stoic souls, who weigh
> Life well, and find it wanting, nor deplore;
> But in disdainful silence turn away
> Stand mute, self-centred, stern, and dream no more?

Nevertheless something of the Stoic peeps out in Arnold, in spite of his sense of frustration, of being astray on a darkling plain, and of the nostalgia which he could express so hauntingly. To be sure, to go through life

> Still nursing the unconquerable hope,
> Still clutching the inviolable shade

would preclude acceptance. Yet in the sonnet which detonates in our ears the most awkwardly cacophanous line ever passed by a good poet,

> Who prop, thou ask'st, in these bad days my mind?

it is Epictetus to whom he refers, together with Homer and Sophocles, the last because he saw life steadily and saw it whole. And though Arnold was far too involved with the Hebraic-Hellenic opposition, each ethos having for him its own strenuousness or excitement, in 'Resignation', the passage ushered in by the aching regret, not acceptance, that

> The world in which we live and move
> Outlasts aversion, outlasts love

goes on:

> And though Fate grudge to thee and me
> The Poet's rapt security,
> Yet they, believe me, who await
> No gifts from Chance, have conquered Fate.
> They, winning room to see and hear,
> And to men's business not too near,
> Through clouds of individual strife
> Draw homeward to the General Life.

That roughly ravels together several strands of Stoical feeling. But Arnold's Stoicism was a flickering state of being, though it might be argued that his 'something not ourselves making for righteousness' is not unlike the brooding divinity of Marcus Aurelius. On the other hand, he could not advocate living according to Nature, since he insisted that 'Nature and man can never be fast friends'. Yet the later Victorian age still clung to more than a shred of the ancient wisdom, if Huxley is any evidence; it was, we are made aware, largely against the general sense of his day that he made his famous antithesis of the cosmic process and the ethical process—a flat denial of all that Stoicism stands for. Yet his sympathy with the 'noble and sane' men who built it up, made him consider their system at some length.[14]

The energetic, battling early Victorians, then, did not find their account in Stoic tranquillity, nor did the mid-Victorians on the emotional surge of their social and scientific prosperity, modified by uneasy twinges of doubt. Nor did it much appear when disillusion began to creep in with the realisation that Utopia was not just round the corner. There is little trace of it in the 'nineties, in Francis Thompson, say, or in Dowson and the Rhymers' Club generally. But if we do not find much in the Georgian poets either, it is extremely significant that by far the most popular poem of the time, read by millions, was Kipling's

'If', which is nothing if not a street version of Campion's
'The Man of Life Upright'. One aspect of it, certainly,
came out in Housman, who caressed an item which appears
amongst those scoffingly repudiated by Milton, but which
lies deep in us, and which we label 'the death wish'—
the Stoic doctrine of the open door. Death is a portal
through which man may voluntarily go if he finds he cannot pass his life in self-respect or dignity:

> . . . if your hand or foot offend you
>   Cut it off, lad, and be whole;
> But play the man, stand up and end you,
>   When your sickness is your soul.[15]

With that we are back to the kind of moral statement,
barely emotive, such as we get from *Nosce Teipsum*. When
a theme splits up into its morsels, it tends to revert to the
didactic, as though it were no longer part of what men
unthinkingly live by.

If in Housman there is no evocation of an all-embracing
scheme, one great poet of the period, deeply seized of the
vision of an indifferent universe, returned to a religious
apprehension related to Stoicism. Hardy's was perhaps an
inverted Stoicism, lacking any trace of human pride, hardly
suggesting endurance. The Eternal process goes on; the
'unweeting Mind' is

> . . . purposive
> Yet superconscious; a Clairvoyancy
> That knows not what It knows, yet works therewith.

Man can do little of himself to fit into the process; we are
lived, as Groddeck might say, by an It:

> So the Will heaves through Space, and moulds the times
> With Mortals for Its fingers! we shall see
> Again men's passions, virtues, visions, crimes,
>   Obey resistlessly
> The mutative, unmotived, dominant Thing
> Which sways in brooding dark their wayfaring![16]

The Dynasts, from which those extracts are taken, is largely
a set of variations on this theme. Hardy was permeated
with it, but in 'Nature's Questioning' he at least suggests
the possibility that 'some high Plan betides', and that man
is 'the Forlorn Hope over which achievement strives'.
But no one, I think, will argue that statements so neutral
are such as man in general can live by. They can hardly
constitute a public theme.

Has the sense of being which I have called Stoicism any
validity to-day? It was once, obviously, expressive of a
general state of feeling; and it surely must mean something that the bulk of my quotations have turned out to be
among the best-known, the most responded to, even now,
in the canon of our poetry. Lately, however, the idea of
Stoic acceptance has seemed to incite to rebellion, more
than to mere rejection, if this is not to misinterpret Mr
Robert Graves's poem 'Certain Mercies', which opens:

> Now must all satisfaction
> Become mere mitigation
> Of an accepted curse?

Must we henceforth be grateful, he asks angrily in the last
stanza,

> That each new indignity
> Defeats only the body,
> Pampering the spirit
> With obscure merit?[17]

Mr Graves is revolted. Mr Dylan Thomas, again, expressed the same rebellion in a vigorously combative villa-
nelle:

> Do not go gentle into that good night,
> Old age should turn and rave at close of day;
> Rage, rage, against the dying of the light.[18]

It is not enough for either that his mind to him should be
a kingdom, that in his soul he should be free. Both are
saying, rather, *La résignation, c'est la défaite de l'âme.*

Are these poems symptomatic? Perhaps there is no longer a general state of being which we can call Stoical to which the poet is bound to respond. If so, one of the reasons may be, as Sir George Rostrevor Hamilton suggests, that man is no longer proud of himself. The jest and riddle of the world? Yes; but he is not prone to see himself in any dazzling glory. No doubt the individual's sense of his dignity is not altogether absent in his daily living, nor some sort of subconscious affirmation that he is what he is, or what he creates; and no doubt there are present certain other intuitions which go to make up the body of what I have with deliberately hazy definition called Stoicism. But they seem to have lost their imaginative basis. The fragmentation of knowledge, which we all deplore while we all so busily further it, has splintered any sense of an eternal order which the average man can hold on to. That old anchorable rock, the certainty that man's thought is free, is dissolving away under the acid of psychoanalysis, or the happy irresponsibility of Behaviourism (I am speaking of how these things appear to the general lay mind). Can man think as he will? Can he will what he is to think? The old dilemma overshadows us with a new insistence. Contradictorily, in the urgency of the atomic age, we feel that far from being governed by some all-pervasive Spirit of the Universe, we are ourselves responsible for the future of man. In any event we are being shaken off from some of the old structures that helped to sustain our emotions in the past. What with the drastic revisions of man's thought—relativity, time concepts and so on, with which as yet the ordinary man cannot grapple, and existentialist *angst*, we have no secure foundation. As a contemporary poet, Mr Gerald Walker puts it:

> The inner world and the outer won't join up.
> The past is a weight about the future's neck.
> Thought won't translate into action—
> At least it won't be translated readily—
> And yet, how else can it be propagated?

Are all old civilisations a sort of priesthood
Building a wall against the world outside them? . . .

. . . Thought sees the world pass from Reality to Dream,
From Dream back to Reality—and sees them both confused
With the ebb of light and darkness and the arrows of great birds
Passing like flights of angels, like another shape of Destiny . . .[19]

The theme may be general enough, but the lines have not
the ring of public utterance. There is not enough there to
be grasped with the intuitive certainty that must accom-
pany, if it cannot always inspire, a poetic transmutation of
anything resembling the Stoic attitude. This has been
possible whenever it has corresponded with the gropings
of the common man: then poets, by the peculiar faculty
which makes them such, have been able to give an assured
value and a fresh liveliness to some of the assumptions on
which men based their way of being. But now? We ask
the question, and Mr Auden answers it in his most cheer-
ful tone:

> . . . however much we may like
> The stoic manner in which
> The classical authors wrote,
> Only the young and the rich
> Have the nerve or the figure to strike
> The lacrimae rerum note.[20]

Stoicism, in fact, in any grand shape, seems to have
petered out. Obviously it can no longer stand, in anything
like its old form, as an intuitive philosophy of life: elements may remain embedded in such diverse attitudes as
Christianity, Communism or Existentialism. Yet even if
split up, it lingers, here and there, as part of it must if we
are to live at all. Not only Mr Alan Ross but Mr Hamish
Henderson has voiced the simplest aspect:

> Endure, endure. There is as yet no solution
> And no short cut, no escape, and no remedy but our human iron,[21]

but thus stated it is only Mr Graves's prison-house comfort. It can no longer carry the implications that it used to,

E

and so cannot exert the poetic pressure that engenders the kind of poetry that springs only from intuitive vision. Mr Graves, we see, is impatient; but the disease goes deeper than that. There is no solid background of generally accepted attitudes or, as Mr Spender suggests, there is a 'loss of continuity'. It is not knowing to what we may be tending, or what we essentially are; or perhaps a lack of relation between the communal and the individual. Stoicism is no holdfast in this age of anxiety, and it would seem to some at least of the younger poets to-day that all the achievement possible is very faintly to trust the smaller hope. Or so it would seem from Mr Anthony Woodhouse's 'Song at Twilight':

> We must go on from here,
> Time has no turning—
> Carry what we have learnt
> Since there is no unlearning.
> The bridge behind is down.
>
> The bridge behind is down,
> The canyon-crack of knowing
> Divides us now from spring,
> And soon where we are going
> Darkness will come, and snow.
>
> Darkness will come, and snow,
> The nightfall of the year—
> And hoping against reason
> To find some kinder season
> We must go on from here.[22]

Such is the fading Stoicism with which he faces the twilight of a civilisation.

Can there be more? Is it possible to find some cross-fertilisation such as Pope attempted? Or some integration into something still more universal such as Wordsworth triumphantly achieved? Possibly. For man has a longing for a sense of eternal order, for fitting in with a scheme of things he can see the point of. Thus it may be that his

common impulses, together with a general acceptance of
the human situation, may formulate themselves in some
fashion akin to the one I have been discussing. If so, it will
crop up, as it used to in poets who are widely read, and are
hailed as great by the commonalty, not perhaps on account
of the poetic qualities we now 'evaluate', but because they
brought to public themes a continually renewed vitality.

CHAPTER III

SCIENTISM I

THE story of poetry and scientism—by which I mean the impact of science on the lay mind—during the last three hundred years, makes up the oddest comedy of personal relations. Poetry has from time to time come out with declarations of honest respect for science, allied with an eager curiosity, growing at times to a warm, pulsing admiration for the fellow as the opener of magic doors on to reality, or the conjurer who will bring everything desirable out of a bountiful hat. Poetry has even fallen prostrate before him, as when Allan Ramsay described the scientist as a god-like man mounting to the skies;[1] or again poetry may defiantly stake out his claim as being, in the words of Shelley, 'the centre and circumference of all knowledge, apprehending all science';[2] or, as Wordsworth put it, 'the breath and finer spirit of all knowledge, the impassioned expression which is in the countenance of all science'.[3] These are varied by a somewhat cavalier acceptance of science as a person who does not after all matter very much; or by a passionate friendship where the two swing along together hand in hand; or a fascination turning to a horrified revulsion, an utter rejection, not only of what science does, but of the kind of creature he is. Sometimes there is a friendly wave of the hand, as to someone you pass on the other side of the road, as, for instance, in Byron's light-hearted salute to astrophysics:[4]

When Newton saw an apple fall, he found
   In that slight startle from his contemplation—
'Tis said (for I'll not answer above ground
   For any sage's creed or calculation)—

A mode of proving that the earth turn'd round
In a most natural whirl called 'gravitation';
And this is the sole mortal who could grapple,
Since Adam, with a fall, and with an apple.*

But the difficulty with this genial relationship is that science refuses to remain the same person; and Mr Auden has thought it friendly to let Byron know that the

Excessive love for the non-human faces
That lives in hearts from Golder's Green to Teddington
[Is] all bound up with Einstein, Jeans, and Eddington.[5]

Yet now, alas, it looks as though the relationship might have to be broken; for when to-day we, the laymen, turn to the popularisations of at any rate physical science we are faced by a series of abstractions, of conjectures; with statements that it is best to regard so and so as such because to do so is mathematically convenient. In Mr Auden's phrase, 'Fate is no longer a fiat of Matter, but a freedom of Mind.'[6] We may, for instance, plunge into Jeans's *The New Background of Science*, as deep as to that part of the chapter on Indeterminacy, where he discussed whether it is better to regard the universe as made up of electrons or of waves. He favoured waves, although

The waves do not admit of representation in space and time, and so cannot be said to possess any physical reality.

Yet [he goes on] in spite of the want of physical reality, this wave picture is in many ways more true to nature, and so is presumably more fundamental, than the particle picture which depicts nature as concrete objects existing in space and time.

What is the poet to do with that? Will he find comfort in Professor Dirac's equation for the propagation of electron waves?

$$\left(E_1 \frac{d}{dx} + E_2 \frac{d}{dy} + E_3 \frac{d}{dz} + E_4 \frac{d}{d\tau} - m \right) \psi = 0$$

Equals zero! Alas yes, so far as the poet is concerned.

* Incidentally a brilliant flash forward to the twentieth-century conception of gravitation—unless, as Dr E. F. Caldin suggests to me, it was some long-abandoned Cartesian notion of vortices in a continuous material fluid.

It was all very well for Dryden, in mid-seventeenth century to write:

> A man should be learned in several sciences, and should have a reasonable philosophic, and in some measure a mathematical head, to be a complete and excellent poet,[7]

but what can the poet do now that the scientists themselves can be learned in only a fragment of one single science? Besides, as we know, the whole procedure of science and poetry are diverse, the scientist in the main going forward by analysis, by measurement, by a severely conditioned intellectual process, separating the unlike; whereas poetry is achieved through synthesis, by abolishing measurement, by uniting unlikes, by not too soon channelling the intellectual processes. Even where the matter is comparatively simple the wary poet will shy off, as Dryden himself did in actual practice. For, interested though this F.R.S. was in science, when he wrote in *Annus Mirabilis*:

> Instructed ships shall sail to quick commerce,
> By which remotest regions are allied,

he left it to a footnote to explain that ships were to be 'instructed' 'by a more exact measure in longitude'. For this he was to be reproved by Dr Johnson:

> It had better become Dryden's learning and genius [he gravely wrote], to have laboured science into poetry, and have shewn, by explaining longitude, that verse did not refuse the ideas of philosophy.[8]

But Dryden was a great poet, and knew what poetry could could not do. He knew, as Eramus Darwin said in one of his charming if naïf discourses with his bookseller, that 'Poetry admits of but few words expressive of very abstract ideas, whereas Prose abounds with them.'[9]

For the poet, of whatever kind, must at some level or other deal with the sensuous. Everybody knows the famous passage in the Preface to *Lyrical Ballads*:

If the labours of Men of science should ever create any material revolution, direct or indirect, in our condition, and in the impressions which we habitually receive, the Poet . . . will be ready to follow the steps of the Man of science, not only in those general indirect effects, but he will be at his side, carrying sensation into the midst of the objects of science itself. The remotest discoveries of the Chemist, the Botanist, or Mineralogist, will be as proper objects of the Poet's art as any upon which it can be employed. . . .

Well and good; but the proviso at once follows:

. . . if the time should ever come when these things shall be familiar to us, and the relations under which they are contemplated by the followers of these respective sciences shall be manifestly and palpably material to us as enjoying and suffering beings.

By Wordsworth's day the poets' attitude towards science had gone through several phases, and we shall be able to distinguish certain clear lines. But science at any time must be important to the poet wherever it is so to the non-scientific man; and it has its importance to the latter on two main counts, firstly and obviously where 'the Man of science' creates such material revolutions as affect our condition—which he has done abundantly in the realm of technology: think only of medicine or transport; and secondly as to the impressions we habitually receive, if only the smell of petrol in our fields, the noisy shudderings of the mechanical drill, sky signs, the sense of speed, and so on. But science has been of fundamental importance to the poet only when it has transformed man's idea of himself or his place in the universe. It is the all-embracing vision that matters.

It would seem that there are various stages in the process of scientism being absorbed into poetry. When some new discovery, in the sense of some generalisation, large or not so universal, is made, the first impulse of the poet seems to be to impart this knowledge which has excited him, make it a public theme. There is, then, a didactic phase, no longer, however, considered respectable, and at any rate possible only so long as the scientist can convey what he means in words, eschewing equations. As the ideas become more familiar they tend to produce descriptive poetry; the reader is expected to be at home with the ideas, and is being helped to co-ordinate them with living. So far, perhaps, no great poetry is produced, though the theme has become public; or, rather, science has not entered into great poetry. What we are after, of course, is not the versifying of scientific statements, but the absorbing by the general mind of scientific ideas or technological achievements, so that the poet can use them as symbols or imagery for the purpose of expression, communication, or finally, creation.

But let us first for a moment hear a minor poet trying to labour science into poetry, to carry sensation into the midst of the objects of science, to make the abstract sensuous, to wit Falconer in *The Shipwreck*. After the storm, the seamen are taking the sun:

> The pilots now their rules of art apply,
> The mystic needle's devious aim to try.
> The compass plac'd to catch the rising ray,
> The quadrant's shadows studious they survey.
> Along the arch the gradual index slides,
> While Phoebus down the vertic circle glides.
> Now, seen on ocean's utmost verge to swim,
> He sweeps it vibrant with his nether limb . . .
> Then through the chiliads triple maze they trace
> [That is, they consult their logarithmic tables.]
> Th'analogy that proves the magnet's place.

Whatever poetry may be, it is certainly not that! Yet, for all we know, it was for the scientific glimpse as much as for the description of the storm and wreck that the poem was immensely popular in its own day.

Obviously the difficulty of poetry in giving utterance to scientism is enormous, and that is largely because poetry and science are both concerned to explore reality. And

though the reality may be one, it doesn't look like it at
first glance. Pure science describes, and elucidates, in a
realm so different from that of poetry (at least from one
point of view) that now, certainly, it seems to be with-
drawing into regions where poetry cannot reach it. Yet if
science is to have any virtue for ordinary men it must be
imaginatively put before them:

> For speculation turns not to itself
> Till it hath travelled, and is married there
> Where it may see itself.[10]

But to-day, when the idea of the universe seems to depend
upon the choice of an equation, when the scientist has with
a vengeance 'Bid mystery to mathematics fly', for speculation to be married to poetry, where it can see itself,
doesn't seem feasible. Even if the two parties are pursuing,
not different truth, but different aspects of truth, the
immediate realities that Science and Poetry probe into are
different; different too is the way they go about it, even
if each works largely through intuition—though with
science, it would seem, not continuously as in poetry, but
at great decisive moments; with Archimedes in his bath,
Newton in his orchard, Darwin on *The Beagle*, and latterly
Einstein, Bohrs and others. It certainly is a false dicho-
tomy to say, as one still hears it said in respectable quarters,
that the scientist pursues truth and the artist, the poet,
beauty. Both pursue truth, searching for actuality and
relationship, and both arrive at beauty. (And, parentheti-
cally, is the satisfaction the scientist feels in achieving a
perfect statement of truth, so far as he has discovered it,
in essence different from the pleasure which fulfils the
artist when he presents the truth so far as it has come to
him at that moment?) Beauty, moreover, is in the eye of
the beholder: it is the reaction of the layman in either
sphere. It is he who recognises it. It is not the goal of the
explorer, for whom beauty is an accidental, or if you prefer,
incidental gift of the gods. And why, perhaps, poetry

directly about science is nearly always of the second order
at best, is because the poet has accepted the scientist's
exploration of truth instead of furthering his own. He has
subdued himself to the material the scientist works in,
instead of adventuring into his own reality.

Sometimes one hears that science and poetry are incompatible; that they are not only opposed methods of arriving
at the nature of being, but that the very bases of their
assumptions are radically apart; and that science, after
all, has no concern with value, which is the ultimate
raison d'être of poetry. The problem is hoary. To-day some
suggest, as does Professor Douglas Bush, that poetry and
religion are fighting a forlorn battle against the dehumani-
sing attacks made upon humanity by the scientists.
Flourishing the sword he quotes Mr Gerald Heard's dic-
tum that 'Newton banished God from nature, Darwin
banished him from life, Freud drove him from the last
fastness, the soul.'[11] We may wonder whether God, 'or
whatever name he may be called by', can so easily be
evicted by any advance in scientific knowledge, for still the
mystery of existence remains; and scientists themselves, so
far as a layman can judge, are beginning to wonder how
far scientific 'facts' may be ideal constructs of their own
minds. Now that 'Physic from metaphysic begs defence'
the days are past when science can be regarded as the dull
mechanic exercise of measuring and weighing. The question appears to be, with the scientists also, What is it,
essentially, that we are measuring and weighing and pre-
dicting about? If poetry—and philosophy in a different
way—is concerned with the 'why' of things, and science
with the 'how', the difference between the two is not ultimately very clear. When the scientist has answered the
question 'Why do the wheels go round?' by explaining
'how' they go round, a new why raises its importunate
head. 'Why the how?' And again—a difficulty of communication here—will a mind habituated to one realm
find the other impenetrable? As Miss Bodkin puts it:

That the reader may participate in the truth of scientific statement, he must be intellectually competent in the technique through which the terms mediate between sensuous experience and a system of abstract relations; that he may participate in the truth of poetic speech he must be emotionally responsive to the technique through which attitudes and imagery of sensuous experience are evoked to constitute a new imaginative whole.[12]

How, we ask, is the poet to bridge this chasm? How can he make scientism a public theme? It is not as though the poet were concerned with the kind of 'sensuous experience' Miss Bodkin postulates for establishing the scientist's 'abstract relations'. That is the real crux, for I do not think that the most appalling barrier lies in the different use of language, incompatible approaches to words, as Dr I. A. Richards insists. He argues that science will handle language to 'indicate' and 'characterise', using it as little as possible to 'realise', that is, to 'intuitively apprehend'; it will avoid appraisal of values, though it may seek help from words that influence.[13] But, we all agree, it is precisely with values that poetry is concerned; it strives to influence the reader, allowing 'indication' and 'characterisation' to enter only as small elements, its end being emphatically 'realisation', so the gap would seem unbridgeable. Mr D. G. James, on the other hand, pleads that language, 'which began as an imaginative thing', continues in our own day, in varying degrees, as an 'imaginative as well as an intellectual thing'.[14] The scientist also has to use metaphor, he hopefully suggests. But how rarely he does it! Sir William Bragg, it is true, told us, in speaking of glass as distinct from crystal, that 'the molecules of the glass are not quite satisfied: they are trying all the time to substitute order for disorder'; and that 'the molecules lay themselves up against one another for good and form the crystalline pattern':[15] but we seldom find writing so vivid, and indeed we might not be deeply moved if some Erasmus Darwin were to contemplate a rapturous poem on the loves of the nuclei. Nevertheless, hope must not be altogether abandoned, and Mr James continues:

> Besides, there is an unbroken line along which the mind may move from the bleakest generalisation to ideas deeply realised ... between the poet and the scientist there is no gap or discontinuity of mind; their union is an ideal which beckons, or should beckon, the poet of a scientific age.

True! But though one may see a beckoning finger, one may be despairingly unable to answer the call.

The difficulty lies much more in the fact that—and here Dr Richards is on much surer ground—the knowledge science has yielded up after centuries of arduous struggle (man hoping that it would tell him how to live), has tricked him.

> Now he has to face the fact that the edifices of supposed knowledge, with which he has so long buttressed and supported his attitudes, will no longer stand up, and, at the same time, he has to recognise that pure knowledge is irrelevant to his aims, that it has no *direct* bearing upon what he should feel, or what he should attempt to do.[16]

That, however, is not so drastically final as it sounds; 'direct' is the operative word; for perhaps a new sense of being in man—the dire rout of his old ideas of personality, the replacement of his experienced notions of time and space by that of a time-space continuum, and so on—if not 'buttressing his attitudes', is certainly affecting his sense of himself, and so poetry. In so far as these things can nourish public themes, they will influence man's values, that is, what he should feel, or what he should attempt to do. But empirically gained knowledge is often felt only as a bar to human vision; the scientist is inveigling man up the wrong street. As Emily Dickinson put it —to stray for a moment out of our islands:

> ... nature is a stranger yet;
> The ones that cite her most
> Have never passed her haunted house,
> Nor simplified her ghost.

> To pity those that know her not
> Is helped by the regret
> That those who know her, know her less
> The nearer that they get.[17]

So that with many poets to-day, Mr Dylan Thomas, for example, we get no hint of science, though Miss Kathleen Raine uses biological imagery. We are at the stage of indifference, perhaps more, not merely shunning, but sometimes clearly antagonistic. For some, then, science, far from enlightening, has weakened and constricted man's vision of the simplest things. It must be utterly cast out. So Mr Padraic Colum in a poem 'The Tulips':

> An age being mathematical, these flowers
> Of linear stalks and spheroid blooms were prized
> By men of wakened, speculative minds . . .
> The Tulips were the light's receptacles.

> The gold, the bronze, the red, the bright-swart Tulips
> No emblem they for us who no more dream
> Of mathematics burgeoning to light
> With Newton's prism and Spinoza's glass,
> Or Berkeley's ultimate Invisible Pure Fire, . . .

For him a kind of Hermetic realisation seems more appropriate; and he prefers to regard the tulips

> as possessed
> Of fieriness to make them flowers fit
> To go with vestments red at Pentecost.[18]

Hermetic: the word takes us back to Elizabethan and Jacobean days, when there was enough palpable scientism to allow the poets to exhibit the didactic, and even the descriptive phase. But at that period we are faced, somewhat confusingly, with two kinds of science, which the Elizabethans themselves did not clearly distinguish: the post-Baconian kind which we now call science, and the earlier Hermetic (which was creative), together with the astrological (which was deterministic), all of which we might call, generally, Paracelsian. This latter figures largely in poetic thought, at least in poetic symbolism; it is almost wholly this kind of science which weaves through the earlier poems of Donne; and it appears considerably at least as late as Henry Vaughan, who was, of course, under the spell of his brother Thomas's Hermetic writings. Sometimes it is difficult to determine which system is being appealed to, as when Marvell in 'The Definition of Love' speaks of parallels, the conjunction of the moon, and opposition of the stars. The pointer is ambiguous; and, whether Marvell was conscious of it or not, his image in 'The Garden' of 'a green thought in a green shade' is referable to the *benedicta viriditas* of the alchemists, the greenness in which the Spirit of God inhabits the vegetable universe. That curious anthology of poems, *Theatrum Chemicum Britannicum*, which Elias Ashmole brought out in 1652, reveals entirely such imagery—though indeed it hardly achieves poetry save in an isolated line or so. It continued to recur, in, for example, Blake; it was there in Kipling's later work, and we find it to-day in Dr Edith Sitwell's *The Shadow of Cain*.

This, however, I must leave aside: the science I would wish to treat of here is of the post-Baconian sort. We find this gradually emerging, disentangling itself, as when in *Orchestra*, a poem built on mediaeval circles and correspondences, Sir John Davies, in a brief parenthesis, admits the existence of so absurd a notion as the Copernican:

> . . . some wits enriched with learning's skill,
> Say heaven stands firm and that the earth doth fleet,
> And swiftly turneth underneath their feet.

But the process is better exemplified by that once widely read book Joshua Sylvester's *Devine Weekes and Workes*, not only Englished from Du Bartas, but, one might say, Anglicised. As with most of the writing at this period, it seems to us an intractable hodge-podge of the mediaeval and the modern, Sylvester, for example, at times turning

'studious Platonist', never doubting the viability of the
notion of the four elements. In the following passage, however, he is on the level of general observation, such as,
being actual, allures the poet. He is explaining 'Why the
Sea receiveth no increase of all the Waters that fall
therein':

> ... notwithstanding, all these Streams that enter
> In the Main Sea, do naught at all augment her:
> For that, besides that all these Floods in one,
> Match'd with great *Neptune*, seem as much as none;
> The Sun (as erst I said) and Windes withall,
> Sweeping the sur-face of the Brinie-Ball,
> Extracts as much still of her humours thin,
> As weeping Aire, and welling Earth pours in.[19]

It errs a little, perhaps, on the side of vagueness, and is
sheer galumphing copy-book didactics.

Drayton, in his disquisition on astronomy in *The Man
in the Moone*, also to us an oddly assorted compendium of
astrology and old-fashioned astronomy mingling with the
new, seems as much more definite than Sylvester as he is
the better poet. We may look at him for a moment respect-
ing the ecliptic. Phoebe is speaking:

> Yet in my selfe had I not Genuine Fire,
> When the grosse Earth decided hath the space,
> Betwixt the full Orbe and my Brother's Face;
> Though I confesse much lessned by my light,
> I should be taken utterly from sight,
> And for I so irregularly goe
> Therein wise Nature most of all doth show
> Her searchlesse judgement: for did I in all
> Keepe on in that way, which Star-gazers call
> The Lyne Ecliptick, as my glorious Brother
> Doth in his course, one opposite to other;
> Twise every Month, the Eclipses of our light,
> Poore Mortals should prodigiously affright;
> Yet by proportion certainly I move
> In rule of number.[20]

Poetry? Not yet altogether perhaps: nevertheless Drayton, though he does not seem to have undergone a complete experience, in fusing abstract relations with sensuous feeling is reaching towards the generalised vision which moves the poet.

There are, I think, three stages in this particular process. The first where a general rough familiarity can allow of the scientific idea or discovery as illustration, as when Pope can say almost casually.

> And now a bubble burst, and now a world:

or the poet can wrest a simile because it is startling, of which Swift provides an amusing example early in the history of the microscope. He is talking about writers and Grub Street critics in the notorious lines:

> So, Nat'ralists observe, a Flea
> Hath smaller Fleas that on him prey,
> And these have smaller Fleas to bite 'em
> And so proceed *ad infinitum*.[21]

Or the mind can be made to glide from a generality to a definite thing, to gain the vividness precision brings:

> . . . the evening is spread out against the sky
> Like a patient etherized upon a table.[22]

Then there is the second stage, when the scientific thing throws light on, or is naturally used as a symbol for, the something else that a poet is talking about, as we shall find in Blake and Shelley, leading with them to the closer phase of complete digestion by the poetic organs, when 'imagery' is more intimately woven into the poem than the word 'symbol' implies.

It would be convenient first to pursue the particular phase where poetry imparts the facts of empirical knowledge. It was at its least doubting when the Newtonian revelation came: then didacticism received a new impulse, though the poets came more and more to abandon it, the major ones giving us scarcely any examples. Yet that it should be there suggests something relevant to my inquiry. Here we meet the bard, not so much singing what everybody knows, but imparting the knowledge about which he proposes to sing. So didactic poetry permeated, 'over-bilged' as Saintsbury put it, the first half of the eighteenth century, one nameless poet remarking in a preface that 'Of all kinds of poetry the *Didascalic* is the most valuable', an opinion we do not share. There is indeed a vast mass of cosmic or naturalistic poetry at this time, most of which constitutes dull, if not lugubrious reading. The bulk of the works, often written by Fellows of the Royal Society, such as Desaguliers or Henry Baker, brings to mind the talk of that none too lively conversationalist Charles Bovary. It was 'flat as a street pavement, along which strolled commonplace ideas, dressed in their everyday clothes, arousing neither feeling, nor laughter, nor speculation', except perhaps, in our case, the relieving laughter of happing upon the worst couplet in the whole canon of our verse—and then a worse one! But this period gives us scientific poetry so infinitely better that I will give no examples from these of sheer didacticism, and return to the period later to illustrate another portion of my thesis.

For the moment, overleaping even that not unattractive person Dr Charles Armstrong, who achieved some pleasant blank verse in *The Art of Preserving Health*, though he confessed that it was hard

> in clear and animated song
> Dry philosophic precepts to convey,

we may go straight to that strange, and to me, I must confess, sympathetic figure, Erasmus Darwin. He, it would seem to the layman, enjoys, or at least enjoyed, some status as a scientist; moreover he really thought about poetry, and within limits, well. Mere Linnaean classification was not enough for him. He ardently wished

> . . . to enlist Imagination under the banner of Science; and to lead her votaries from the looser analogies, which dress out the

F

imagery of poetry, to the stricter ones which form the ratiocination of philosophy.[23]

Although Coleridge 'absolutely nauseated' his poetry, it
can, if approached without prejudice, be read with enjoyment. He is at least ingenious. Take him, for instance,
talking about the continual regeneration of life, under the
heading of wedding 'the enamoured Oxygene to Light':

> —Hence plastic Nature, as Oblivion whelms
> Her fading forms, repeoples all her realms;
> Soft Joys disport on purple plumes unfurl'd,
> And Love and Beauty rule the willing world.[24]*

Darwin, however, was perfectly aware of the difficulty of
'poetising' science, of transcending description and achieving imagery. When his bookseller asks him 'Then a
simile should not very accurately resemble the subject?'
he answers, 'No, it would then become a philosophical
analogy, it would be ratiocination instead of poetry.'
Analogy, alas, flares out luridly in *The Loves of the Plants*,
where ratiocination is a little difficult to find. A typical
enough example is his handling of the Gloriosa Superba,
which, the notes tell us, contains in the flower six stamens
(the males) and one pistil (the female). Three of the stamens
mature first, and some days afterwards, the other three.
This is what Imagination may do when enlisted under the
banner of Science:

> When the young Hours amid her tangled hair
> Wove the fresh rose-bud and the lily fair,
> Proud GLORIOSA led *three* chosen swains,
> The blushing captives of her virgin chains.—
> —When Time's rude hands a bark of wrinkles spread
> Round her weak limbs, and silvered o'er her head,
> Three other youths her riper years engage,
> The flatter'd victims of her wily age.[24]

---

* The passage is not uninteresting from the point of view of aesthetics,
with its reference to 'plastic Nature', as though Darwin were a disciple of
Shaftesbury.

But imagination does not stop there: it leads Darwin, in an unusual digression, to tell, pathetically, the story of Ninon de l'Enclos.

> So with her wane of beauty Ninon won
> With fatal smiles her gay unconscious son . . .

In the event, it is, I fear, merely very funny. It might be pleaded for Darwin that he was fulfilling what used to be considered one of the functions of poetry, to make useful facts memorable; but what he was trying to do was something far more important in poetry, namely to universalise. He failed, as he knew, since he makes his bookseller say to him, 'Your verses, Mr Botanist, consist of *pure description*. I hope there is some *sense* in the notes.' But it is clear that sheer scientific didacticism is as unprofitable as didacticism always is in poetry; and with Darwin's we have, I think, the last serious attempt. At all events, I drop that thread, culling only a recent example from Professor Douglas Bush:

> Twinkle, twinkle little star,
> I don't wonder what you are;
> For by the spectroscopic ken
> I know that you are hydrogen.

Mnemonically, at least, that is perfect.

Yet there is still poetry that is very nearly didactic. Take for example Mr Auden absorbing depth-psychology. In him Groddeck has been the chief imaginative influence, though one does not forget the moving poem 'In Memory of Dr Freud', 'no more a person now, but a whole climate of opinion'. *The Orators* is permeated with it, *The Ascent of F6* partly rests on it. I want, however, to take the lines, well-known enough, which conclude his volume *Poems*; and which he has at long last entitled 'Petition':

> Sir, no man's enemy, forgiving all
> But will his negative inversion, be prodigal:
> Send to us power and light, a sovereign touch
> Curing the intolerable neural itch,

The exhaustion of weaning, the liar's quinsy,
And the distortions of ingrown virginity.
Prohibit sharply the rehearsed response
And gradually correct the coward's stance;
Cover in time with beams those in retreat
That, spotted, they turn though the reverse were great;
Publish each healer that in city lives
Or country houses at the end of drives;
Harrow the house of the dead; look shining at
New styles of architecture, a change of heart.

That is very complex. I am not sure that I understand it all, though the main lines are plain. But here we have scientism at the stage we meet with in the early eighteenth century, the stage of didacticism through description.

To turn then from the didactic aspect, I would glance for a moment at what poetry has done, not with the science concerned with generalising what may be found in some delimited field, but with its practical achievements; to technology, which does after all give us things 'manifestly and palpably material to us as enjoying and suffering beings'. Common objects naturally appear in poetry as part of the stuff of common life, with or without some slight overtone—'the taxi throbbing, waiting', aircraft, power stations, radio sets—and all the thousand toys which assault us in our daily lives. They are seldom symbolic, because, as with 'pure' science, some time must elapse before they can produce a response as natural as trees, or motherhood, or war. As Professor Day Lewis has said:

> . . . ideas are not material for the poetic mind until they have become commonplaces for the 'practical' mind . . . Scientific data must first be assimilated by the general consciousness and integrated with the whole environment, then they must undergo a further process of digestion in the individual poetic organs.[25]

Let me illustrate. The railway, for fairly obvious reasons, is the object that seems most to have entered into our poetry, but not immediately as metaphor or symbol; it was long after 1830 before Tennyson could refer to the world spinning for ever 'down the ringing grooves of change' even if he did err as to the exact structure of railway lines, for here too there seems to be three stages. The earliest use known to me, but here analogically, almost by way of an 'emblem', is inscribed on a tombstone of 1845 in Ely Cathedral, in verses so charmingly simple that I can't resist quoting some of them here. And besides, they illustrate my argument so happily.

> The Line to heaven by Christ was made
> With heavenly truth the Rails are laid,
> From Earth to Heaven the Line extends,
> To Life Eternal where it ends . . .
>
> God's Love the Fire, his Truth the Steam
> Which drives the Engine and the Train.
> All you who would to Glory ride,
> Must come to Christ, in him abide . . .
>
> Come then poor Sinners, now's the time
> At any Station on the Line.
> If you repent and turn from sin
> The Train will stop and take you in.

No one would have the temerity to claim that as poetry— though I feel Quarles might have liked it. But here we are still in the first stage, though looking shyly towards the second. Mr Day Lewis himself has given an example to illustrate the latter in some lines written in an epithalamium:

> Let us be off. Our steam
> Is deafening the dome.
> The needle in the gauge
> Points to the long-banked rage
> And trembles there to show
> What pressure's below.
> Valve cannot vent the strain
> Nor iron ribs refrain
> The furnace in the heart.
> Come on, make haste and start

> Coupling-rod and wheel
> Welded of patient steel
> Piston that will not stir
> Beyond the cylinder
> To take in its stride
> A teeming countryside.[26]

That is fairly direct symbolism; but there perhaps Mr Day Lewis is expecting the reader to do too much of the work the poem should be doing for him. Mr Spender, with hints of the third stage, gets closer to fusing the symbol in his poem 'The Midland Express', the 'muscular virtuoso' whom he addresses:

> O juggler of the wheeling towns and stars
> Unpausing even with the night,
> Beneath my lines I read your iron lines
> Like the great art beneath a little life
> Whose giant travelling ease
> Is the vessel of its effort and fatigue.[27]

But the most complete catching up of machinery into the substance of a poem is still Kipling's triumphant 'M'Andrew's Hymn'. Kipling was always boyishly thrilled by technology—though his science tended to the Paracelsian—and he seems to turn naturally to mechanics for imagery as in his 'Hymn of Breaking Strain'. There, however, the treatment is still on the level of analogy. 'M'Andrew' is as different as the track-cyclist's idol from the old bone-shaker. For the 'dour Scots engineer' the engines of his ship completely symbolise the Calvinism of his upbringing:

> Lord, Thou hast made this world below the shadow of a dream,
> An', taught by time, I tak it so—exceptin' always Steam.
> From coupler-flange to spindle-guide I see Thy Hand, O God—
> Predestination in the stride o' yon connectin' rod.
> John Calvin might ha' forged the same—enorrmous certain, slow—
> Ay, wrought it in the furnace-flame—*my* 'institutio'. . . .

Her time, her own appointed time, the rocking link-head bides,
Till—hear that note?—the rod's return whings glimmerin'
    through the guides.
They're all awa'! True beat, full power, the clangin' chorus goes
Clear to the tunnel where they sit, my purrin' dynamoes.
Interdependence absolute, foreseen, ordained, decreed
To work, Ye'll note, at ony tilt an' every rate o' speed.
Fra skylight-lift to furnace-bars, backed, bolted, braced an'
    stayed,
An' singin' like the Mornin' Stars for joy that they are made;
While, out o' touch o' vanity, the sweatin' thrust-block says:
'Not unto us the praise, or man—not unto us the praise!'
Now, a'together, hear them lift their lesson—theirs an' mine:
'Law, Orrder, Duty an' Restraint, Obedience, Discipline!'

There the fusion is almost complete, as it was, in a far
earlier stage of technology, when Southwell wrote 'The
Burning Babe', which one suspects Kipling to have had
in mind when he wrote 'M'Andrew'. Here, in 1596, is
Southwell:

My faultless breast the furnace is, the fuel wounding thorns,
Love is the fire and sighs the smoke, the ashes shames and scorns;
The fuel Justice layeth on, and Mercy blows the coals,
The metal in this furnace wrought are men's defiled souls.

But yet, in both, there is still the strong flavour of direct
analogy; and one may hazard that however good the poet,
technology can never by itself inform a great poem. But
should man make an engine which might completely alter
his relationship with his fellows, stir him so deeply as to
revise the assumptions by which he lives, then great poetry
might be engendered. The atom-bomb is a case in point:
it has made a hideous gargoyle of the figure of man as it
exists for the imaginative man or woman. Whence one
terrifying poem, *The Shadow of Cain*, which Dr Edith Sitwell would not mind being called terrible, its implications
are so torturing. I quote one stanza:

We did not heed the Cloud in the Heavens shaped like the hand
Of Man . . . But there came a roar as if the Sun and Earth had
    come together—
The Sun descending and the Earth ascending
To take its place above . . . the Primal Matter
Was broken, the womb from which all life began,
Then to the murdered Sun a totem pole of dust arose in memory
    of Man.

You may say that this all refers to the use man makes of
science rather than to technology; but in the whole poem
imagery is drawn from the sciences, anthropology, and
what Lombroso and Havelock Ellis had to say, modern
science mingling with the Paracelsian. And after all, the
poet ultimately deals in magic.

Yet men, and therefore poets, have always been curious
not only about what science had to tell them, but also about
what it could do for them. Early in our own literary history
Chaucer mastered the astrolabe, though Spenser shame-
facedly confessed to Gabriel Harvey that he was no hand
at 'the Canons, Tables, and instruments of astronomy'.
What seems most to have stirred some of the Elizabethans
was the promise science offered them of man's conquest
over nature. This was the glamour which stirred Marlowe
when in the first act of *Faustus* that hero rapturously
burst out:

    Oh, what a world of profit and delight,
    Of power, of honour and omnipotence
    Is promised to the studious artizan!

and when he dreamed of what he could achieve if grounded
in astrology, enriched with tongues, and well seen in
minerals. It is a foreshadowing of the Baconian vision of
man's limitless power over nature.

It is significant, however, that the poets have not been
much moved by technological achievements. They are
rather like the Chinaman who, when urged by the excited
Englishman to wonder at the first aeroplane that ever flew
over Peking, cast a casual glance up at it and remarked 'I

don't see anything wonderful in it: the thing was designed
to fly, and it flies.' Power, however, did appeal to Erasmus
Darwin. He is entranced by the possibilities; but in his
work steam is not used as imagery. He is still in the descriptive phase, though we will think astoundingly prophetic, remembering that this passage was written in
about 1790:

> Soon shall thy arm, UNCONQUER'D STEAM! afar
> Drag the slow barge, or drive the rapid car;
> Or on wide-waving wings expanded bear
> The flying chariot through the fields of air.
> —Fair crews triumphant, leaning from above,
> Shall wave their fluttering kerchiefs as they move;
> Or warrior bands alarm the gaping crowd,
> And armies shrink beneath the shadowy cloud.[28]

Sometimes, however, you may get a poet delighted by the
appearance of technological objects—pylons, for example,
swinging with huge strides across downland. Mr Francis
Berry is excited by a sports-car:

> Streamlined aluminium chastity—
> O Artemis of the Great West Road,
> Shifting silver secrets as she flies.
> Her tonneaux like the breasts of foam-born
> Cytherean, furnaced in the factory.
> Wheel-wings Juno-wristed: O miracle
>   Of man-made majesty.[29]

But it is the idea, the generalisation that changes man's
notion of himself, that alone can be a theme for great
poetry, not the adventitious aids to living.

For man-made majesty, however 'miraculous', will not
answer the 'why' the poet is for ever asking; it says
nothing about the nature of reality. Wordsworth made the
point clearly enough in his sonnet 'Steamboats, Viaducts
and Railways':

> Motions and Means, on land and sea at war
> With old poetic feeling, not for this,
> Shall ye, by Poets even, be judged amiss!

> Nor shall your presence, howsoe'er it mar
> The loveliness of nature, prove a bar
> To the Mind's gaining that prophetic sense
> Of future change, that point of vision, whence
> May be discovered what in soul ye are . . .

and even Kipling, though responding eagerly to technological feats, at the end of a translation of one of the Odes that Horace neglected to write, thrusts all these things aside, preferring to sink himself 'in thought profound of what the unaltering Gods require'.

CHAPTER IV

SCIENTISM II

I T is probable that in the early seventeenth century the average man did not securely enough feel what the revolution in science implied for the poet to absorb it, or to want to use scientific imagery. It was not of course that the sensuous was changing, but that men's thoughts about it were. As Professor Butterfield tells us, at that time

> in both celestial and terrestrial physics . . . change is brought about, not by new observations or additional evidence in the first instance, but by transpositions that were taking place inside the minds of scientists themselves,[1]

a state of affairs to which the poets, Donne in particular, were sensitive. Not that it would seem, however, that Donne was really interested in science: it served him only so far as accepted concepts formed his imagery, and it was the Paracelsian form of these which inhabited his mind. His lack of real interest in this revolution seems clear from the couplet in *The Second Anniversarie:*

> And one Soule thinks one, and another way
> Another thinks, and 'tis an even lay . . .

Naturally enough anybody who thought at all would be disturbed. For one man, here he was yesterday occupying proudly (when he wasn't remembering to be humble) the centre of a universe in which the planets had been especially created to revolve so as to influence him: now he was a speck on a shred in a system of a vastness that fatigued the imagination. For another man, it might be matter for

75

pride and rejoicing that he was no longer the wretched inhabitant of a *dead* centre at which the light, warmth, colour and music of a glorious universe died out. For in either case would not all this make him behave very differently? Mr D. G. James, indeed, underlining the fact that Bacon's *The Advancement of Learning* was published between *Hamlet* and *Lear*, quite plausibly invites us to believe that the 'New Learning' begot the tremendous questionings of those two plays, as affecting the whole basis of morals.[2] The doubt, the confusion, the attempts to bring the old and new together, to mingle oil and water, went on all through the century, at any rate in the general mind. It made it difficult for the poet to hob-nob with science; and even so late as 1716 or so Prior, who refused to accept the vauntings of the fashionable scientific philosophy, could write in *Alma*:

> For, Dick, if we could reconcile
>   Old Aristotle with Gassendus,
> How many would admire our toil,
>   But yet how few would comprehend us.

By that time, however, something else had happened; there had been created a new vision which penetrated and enchanted the general mind, and issued as a public theme in poetry.

Intermediately, however, poetry was cautious. Not that the aid science might bring to poetry was ignored. As Dr Ian Jack has lately pointed out, Sprat referred to the 'vast Treasure of admirable *Imaginations* which [science] afforded [Bacon], wherewith to express and adorn his thoughts in other matters'.[3] And answering Davenant's *Preface to Gondibert*: 'From *Knowing* much, proceedeth the admirable variety and novelty of Metaphors and Similitudes . . . the want whereof compelleth a Writer to expressions that are either defac'd by time or sullied with vulgar or long use.' Nevertheless, a few satirists apart, the poets on the whole did no more than blandly note that certain import-

ant discoveries had been made, and left their significance
to be revealed later. Thus Dryden (who, as a professing
astrologer, might be allowed to be a little chary), in his
'Epistle to Dr Charleton' merely recorded that:

> The World to Bacon does not onely owe
> Its *present* Knowledge, but its *future* too;
> *Gilbert* shall live, till *Lode-stones* cease to draw
> Or *British* Fleets the boundless Ocean awe.
> And noble *Boyle*, not less in *Nature* seen,
> Than his great *Brother*, read in *States* and *Men*.
> The *Circling* streams, once thought but pools, of blood
> (Whether Life's Fewel or the Bodie's food)
> From dark Oblivion *Harvey's* name shall save;
> While *Ent* keeps all the honour that he gave.

which is, at least, taking his hat off to the scientists. Cowley, however, grapples with the issues. In that splendid
Pindaric galleon, the 'Ode to the Royal Society', after
praising Bacon for chasing Authority out of our sight, and
for breaking the 'scar-crow Deity' Priapus (though what
the god was doing in that shrubbery is not very clear),
he spurs mankind on to pursue science:

> We would be like the Deity
> When Truth and Falshood, Good and Evil, we
> Without the Senses Aid within ourselves would see;
> For 'tis God only who can find
> All Nature in his Mind.

A splendid vindication of experimental work.* Moreover
he goes on to defend all scientific research, however much
'proud' men may despise the investigation of minute
things as 'impertinent, vain and small'—though that did
not prevent poets of later generations, Swift in particular,
from mocking the *virtuosi* who enjoyed the microscope.

But what is important to poets is when scientific discoveries really affect the mind of man in his daily vision,

---

* Even if it was an echo of Telesius, who a century earlier in his *De
Rerum Natura* had attacked those 'who trusted over much in their owne
witte and forgot to look upon the things them selves'. I owe this quotation
to Mr C. S. Lewis.

and thus fertilise his imagination. It happened on a large
scale in the early eighteenth century. The previous one
had become accustomed to the notion of a vast universe;
but mere size is only staggering, and poetry can do little
with it. A startling change came when 'God said "Let
Newton be", and there was light.' It is not going too far
to say that his *Principia* and his *Opticks* were landmarks in
English poetry. The revelation of how the starry heavens
worked, of why the rainbow was what it was, challenged
or created wonder in the minds of men in general, and at
moments made poets out of the most prosy versifiers. The
sense of the whole of actuality, of existence, working
according to understandable universal laws itself constituted the sort of experience which is metre-making. It is
perhaps difficult for us to appreciate that excitement; the
older among us perhaps might compare it with that when
Freud's generalisations brought an almost lucid coherence
into a previously baffling and chaotic realm. At all events
Newton's contemporaries thrilled to an exciting vision that
could serve poetry as a public theme, seeing that poetry
alone could communicate it emotionally. For once at least,
science and the muse went hand in hand. Nor was it a
mere compulsive fashion. A real feeling that man's relation to the universe had been radically adjusted made it,
apparently, a necessity for every poet or poetaster at least
to mention Newton; nobody has had the courage to count
the number of Odes to Newton that signalised his death.
His 'opening of Nature's adamantine gates', as Glover put
it, carried with it a great aura of miraculous beauty, and
Glover goes on:

> Newton demands the muse; his sacred hand
> Shall guide her infant steps; his sacred hand
> Shall raise her to the Heliconian height,
> Where, on its lofty top enthron'd, her head
> Shall mingle with the stars.[4]

A little rhetorical, perhaps; but the marvellous neatness of
the great scheme of things, the wonderful smoothing out

of complexities, freed the imagination, partly no doubt because the Newtonian system seemed finally to cast the great bugbear of Aristotelianism on the rubbish heap. Earlier, both Dryden in his 'Epistle to Dr Charleton' and Cowley in his 'Ode' to Hobbes, had rejoiced in the putting to rout of 'the mighty stagyrite'; and now the new science provided a release from the dubieties of Cartesianism as well. As Thomson said of Newton:

> The heavens are all his own, from the wide rule
> Of whirling vortices and circling spheres
> To their first great simplicity restored.[5]

It was the dazzling beauty of the whole that carried the poets off their feet. Thomson's 'To the Memory of Sir Isaac Newton' is evidence enough for that. Thomson to be sure had his didactic lapses, and, priding himself on scientific accuracy, twice altered his account of watersprings so as to be smartly up to date with the latest theory. But in the passage I shall read he is clearly deeply moved, and if the last line may seem to us to descend to bathos, it may be that it is our own imaginations that are defective.

> Did ever poet image aught so fair,
> Dreaming in whispering groves by the hoarse brook?
> Or prophet, to whose rapture heaven descends?
> Even now the setting sun and shifting clouds,
> Seen, Greenwich, from thy lovely heights, declare
> How just, how beauteous, the refractive law.

And Thomson was only one among a swarm of poets to be so moved. Moreover the whole question of light, of colour, of the prism, chimed admirably with the new interest in landscape painting, and the prevalent addiction to nature poetry. All this, however, has been so brilliantly dealt with by Professor Marjorie Nicolson[6] that I need not enlarge upon it. Nor, apart from the connected theories of vision, and the psychology of the day, did this part of Newton's work greatly affect man's view of himself, or of his place

in the universe. Far more important was the new astronomy, which began to figure in poetry as early as 1709,
with Reynolds, and continued at least until Shelley. This
might indeed affect ethics.

Its first result, however, was a terrific tidal wave of imaginative description, phosphorescent with wonder. Even
Blackmore in *Creation* was galvanised out of his usual hum-
drum versification: but perhaps it was the unduly despised
Mallet who, in *The Excursion*—one of the many cosmic
poems of the period—best gives us a sense of a tremendous
vision, itself an experience, communicable as poetic experience. Divagating on 'the blue profundity of heaven', he
bursts into apostrophe:

> Unfathomable, endless of extent!
> Where unknown suns to unknown systems rise,
> Whose numbers who shall tell? Stupendous host!
> In flaming millions through the vacant hung,
> Sun beyond sun, and world to world unseen,
> Measureless distance, unconceived by thought!
> Awful their order; each the central fire
> Of his surrounding stars, whose whirling speed,
> Solemn and silent, through the pathless void
> Nor change nor error knows.[7]

And here, still, a hundred years later, Shelley, in a not so
different way, and filled with something of the old wonder:

> Below lay stretched the boundless universe!
>   There, far as the remotest line
> That limits swift imagination's flight
> Unending orbs mingled in mazy motion,
>   Immutably fulfilling
>   Eternal Nature's law.
>   Above, below, around,
>   The circling systems formed
>   A wilderness of harmony,
>   Each with undeviating aim
> In eloquent silence through the depths of space
>   Pursued its wondrous way.[8]

That this public theme was metre-making, with all that that implies, is obvious. Even Erasmus Darwin was stirred to a passage which doesn't sully *The Oxford Book of Eighteenth Century Verse*.

And if the telescope provided matter for a new human excitement, so did the microscope. Again and again, in the minor poets of the first forty years of the century, such as John Phillips, Diaper, Samuel Boyse, Moses Browne, Henry Brooke, we find delight in the animalculae, which in their myriads so flatteringly for man extended downwards the Chain of Being. But it was a matter giving rise to quaint fancy rather than imagination, as when Henry Baker, speaking in *The Universe* of the tiniest microscopic creatures, avers that 'they too are pain'd with love;—address the fair.' And as the better poets tended to deplore time wasted on the study of these minimal creatures, since these made no difference to man's place in nature, I spare quotation.

All this fitted in very well with all sorts of popularly held philosophic notions—especially the pervasive Deism of the period; above all, it appealed to the poetic desire for universality. What had really happened was that the eye had been made freshly aware of what was going on in the world of sensation; science had made men look about them more keenly. As Akenside confessed:

> Nor ever yet
> The melting rainbow's vernal-tinctured hues
> To me have shown so pleasing, as when first
> The hand of science pointed out the path
> In which the sunbeams gleaming from the west
> Fall on the wat'ry cloud . . . [9]

and so on. Man's curiosity was aroused, delighted, and satisfied. Yet it was not in the process, the procedures, of science that they were interested; they responded to it only as it pointed out fresh wonders, or illustrated—to use the title of Ray's book—the wisdom of God in the creation.

But the phase could not last. The metaphysical implications, the determinism of the Newton-Locke system,

G

dawned upon men; it was seen to deny the possibility of creative modification, nature itself being no longer 'plastic', but rather, in Whitehead's words, 'a dull affair, soundless, scentless, colourless: merely the hurrying of material, endlessly, meaninglessly'. Science could no longer fructify the imagination of the poet, and he turned elsewhere, to history especially, for revelation of himself. Yet poetry had to a great degree mirrored 'scientism', though, even at its best, this had not, as Coleridge would put it, the 'greatest relish' of poetry, at least for us, who look for the language of poetry to be symbolic. For with these poets nature, the thing described, was itself the symbol—the actuality of purpose, of order, of divine necessitarianism. They were therefore descriptive, and description differs from imagery, which has a reference outside itself; and these poets never came to use the world-without as imagery in this sense. They did not feel the need to.

And as in the course of time the sense of wonder faded, the theme, as mere statement, lost its vitality. Plenty of verse was written on the subject, but in phrases worn dim by vulgar use, with Hermetic imagery creeping back, though without its old implications. It needed integrating with something other; it was no use merely to go back to didacticism in a different department, as Darwin did. It needed further universalising, and this did not occur until Shelley gathered it up in his vision.

Extraordinary efforts have been made in recent years to claim him as a great scientist lost. Whitehead, the phrase is well known, assured us that 'If Shelley had been born a hundred years later, the twentieth century would have seen a Newton among chemists.'[10] But if Shelley had pined to be a chemist—and as a schoolboy his interest had been vividly aroused—there was nothing to prevent him; chemistry was flourishing in his day. Whitehead claimed that the line

The vaporous exultation not to be confined

is the poetic transcript of 'the expansive force of gases',
a notion anyone can acquire without scientific training by
watching the lid on a boiling kettle. He gathered from
Prometheus Unbound the lines Earth utters beginning:

> I spin beneath my pyramid of night
> Which points into the heavens . . .

and declared that 'this stanza could only have been written
by someone with a definite geometrical diagram before
his inward eye': but, as Professor Grabo, himself eager
to enlist Shelley as a scientist, points out, the diagram
would show a cone, not a pyramid, which in all likelihood
comes from Pliny.[11] It is true that, especially in his earlier
days, Shelley was delighted with what science could do
and show: and, of course, it was enormous fun to admini-
ster electric shocks to his sister Hellen. Later, like all
intelligent men, he was aware, as far as the layman can be,
of the goings-on of science; and like all sensible men, he
accepted its main findings so far as he could understand
them. What is more important, he could express them in
imagery. The moon, for example, earth's 'crystal para-
mour' addresses the world:

> Brother, wheresoe'er thou soarest
> I must hurry, whirl and follow
> Through the heavens wide and hollow
> Sheltered by the warm embrace
> Of thy soul from hungry space,
> Drinking from thy sense and sight,
> Beauty, majesty and light . . .[12]

Professor Grabo is entitled to claim that 'warm embrace'
symbolises gravitational force, and that the lines mean that
the gravitational pull of the earth keeps the moon from
flying off into space. That however required no startling
scientific intuition; Blackmore had as much. It is true,
indeed, that Shelley read enthusiastically. He devoured
the scientific articles in the current encyclopaedias, curry-
combed Laplace, Cabanis, Bailly, Cuvier for ideas, steeped

himself in Bacon—but quite happily put Lucretius and
Pliny on a level with these. Yet he was ahead of most poets
by, much sooner than they usually do, fusing the ideas of
his own time into his poetry. Normally—and this is where
Keats was wrong—the findings of science become poetic-
ally usable only when they actually do come into the catalogue of common things, when they are part of common
apprehension. Blake, for example, rabidly anti-Newtonian
though he was, yet made use of his corpuscular theory of
light, and his conception of ether. So in the book of *Los*,
as Miss Nicolson notes:

> Then Light first began: from the fires,
> Beams, conducted by fluid so pure,
> Flow'd round the Immense. Los beheld . . .
> Forthwith, writhing upon the dark void,
> The Back bone of Urizen appear
> Hurtling upon the wind
> Like a serpent! like an iron chain
> Whirling about in the Deep.

> And first from those infinite fires,
> The light that flow'd down on the winds
> He seiz'd, beating incessant, condensing
> The subtil particles in an Orb.

> Roaring indignant, the bright sparks
> Endur'd the vast Hammer, but unwearied
> Los beat on the Anvil, till glorious,
> An immense Orb of fire he fram'd . . .

> . . . till a Form
> Was completed, a Human Illusion
> In darkness and deep clouds involv'd.[13]

Both poets were doing what Thomson and his like had
been trying for, but now in a more personified, more
dramatic, and essentially more poetic way, because they
pierced beyond the visible. And now, too, the notion of the
great universal process was enough part of the general
mind for the poetry that dealt with it to go beyond the
didactic or descriptive phase into the symbolic, the crea-

tively modifying. Shelley was not interested in the mere facts of science. 'You know', he wrote to Peacock, 'I always seek in what I see the manifestation of something beyond the present and tangible object.' He was, in short, a kind of Berkeleyan, talking in 'The Sensitive Plant' of 'this life'

> Where nothing is, and all things seem,
> And we the shadow of a dream;

or saying in 'Mont Blanc';

> The everlasting universe of Things
> Flows through Mind, and rolls its rapid waves
> Now dark—now glittering—now reflecting gloom—
> Now lending splendour, where from secret springs
> The source of human thought its tribute brings
> Of waters.

What exactly is Shelley doing? He is, as Dr Grabo says, attempting 'to unify the universe, to reduce matter and energy to being one principle'.[14] But the intuition came first, and he eagerly seized upon any scientific statement that seemed to support this. Erasmus Darwin perhaps provided fuel for his flame, as when in *The Botanic Garden* he speaks of 'Ens without weight, and substance without shade', or of 'forms sphered in fire'. But to accept that Shelley was so influenced we must agree with Dr Grabo that Darwin was here advancing 'a concept of matter which identifies matter with energy', and that the phrases 'can mean nothing if not descriptive of units of matter which are no more than radiant points of force'. Unluckily, to the simple reader Darwin seems merely to have been amusing himself hugely with the Rosicrucian salamanders, and so forth (as Pope had in *The Rape of the Lock*, so far not claimed for scientism) because he thought it 'to afford proper machinery for a Botanic poem'.* Far more rele-

---

* Adding 'as it is probable, that they were originally the names of hieroglyphic figures representing the elements'. *The Botanic Garden: Apology.*

vant are certain passages Dr Grabo quotes from Davy's *Elements of Chemical Philosophy*, which I will try to condense. Davy argued that all matter was probably ultimately the same in essence, physical points endowed with attraction and repulsion which could be electrically measured. All matter was reducible to particles possessed of motion, which must be an undulation or vibration of the particles about their axes, or a motion round each other. Is this what Shelley was trying to impart at the level of creative poetry when he wrote:

> A sphere, which is as many thousand spheres
> Solid as crystal, yet through all its mass
> Flow, as through empty space, music and light:
> The thousand orbs involving and involved,
> Purple and azure, white and green, and golden,
> Sphere within sphere; and every space between
> Peopled with unimaginable shapes,
> Such as ghosts dream of dwell in the lampless deep.
> Yet each inter-transpicuous, and they whirl
> Over each other with a thousand motions,
> Upon a thousand sightless axles spinning.
> And with the force of self-destroying swiftness
> Intensely, slowly, solemnly roll on . . .
> With mighty whirl the multitudinous orb
> Grinds the bright brook into an azure mist
> Of elemental subtlety, like light . . . [15]

That is magnificent; but surely it is taking the idea beyond empirical science, as you may say was done by Jeans and Eddington in their idealistic hostility to determinism. For, to quote Whitehead again, 'Berkeley, Wordsworth, Shelley, are representative of the intuitive refusal to accept the abstract materialism of science.' Shelley, in fact, would not accept science at all, *as itself*. 'All science', he claims in *A Defence of Poetry*, 'must be referred to poetry.' He sensed what we are now discovering, that, to repeat from Dr Richards, 'man has to recognise that pure knowledge is irrelevant to his aims, that it has no direct bearing upon

what he should feel, or what he should attempt to do'.
Shelley knew at least that knowledge was not enough: 'We
want the creative faculty to imagine that which we know',
he insisted. And:

> The cultivation of those sciences which have enlarged the limits
> of the empire of man over the external world, has, for want of
> the poetical faculty, proportionately circumscribed those of the
> internal world; and man, having enslaved the elements, remains
> himself a slave.[16]

Can then the poet, by making a public theme of science,
foster the imagination which alone can make our knowledge something by which we essentially live? That is the
fundamental question.

So Shelley's last statement invites us to look at the other
side of the story, the estrangement of poetry from science.
I don't think that in the sixteenth and seventeenth centuries there was much reservation, or very much sus-
picion of science, other than in the minds of the satirists
such as Butler, Oldham and Rochester. But already in the
early eighteenth century poetry is getting a little uneasy.
The position is ambiguous, for together with an almost
passionate acceptance of science, an ecstatic plunge into
scientism (that is, science as it filters down to the averagely
interested and averagely lazy layman), there goes a feeling
that science is being too forward in claiming a priority in
the friendly relation, is too eager to be the senior partner.
Gradually a coldness creeps in, a sheer indifference, leading even to a vehement denial that it is decorous to know
the fellow. Poetry was beginning to think that science was
becoming too self-important, taking himself far too seri-
ously. Swift, as an early example, refers contemptuously
to this upstart, laughing about

> A search, no doubt, as curious and as wise
> As virtuosoes' in dissecting flies;[17]

and later has his tremendous fling at the scientists in Book
III of *Gulliver's Travels*.

But it was Blackmore, himself a scientist, a doctor of medicine, and a poet of scientism, who was the first to exhibit a reasoned uneasiness, even in his bulky scientific poem *Creation*. You may, he tells the scientist, give things names, but does this really explain anything? Your 'hows' may get ever more detailed, but are you any nearer the 'why'? Speaking of the heavier bodies, he says bluntly:

> *If some you say, prest with a ponderous load*
> *Of gravity, move slower in their road*
> *Because with weight encumber'd and opprest,*
> *These sluggish orbs th'attractive suns resist;*
> Till you can weight and gravity explain,
> These words are insignificant and vain:[18]

which if not poetry, is at least a protest. He also put into verse his extreme scepticism about Newton's corpuscular theory of light, and the whole then modern theory of vision, which it took Berkeley to grapple with. But here he is scientist more than poet. It is, rather, to Pope that we turn for poetry on the subject. In the *Essay on Man*, for instance, he asks about Newton:

> Could he, whose rules the rapid Comet bind,
> Describe or fix one movement of his Mind?
> Who saw its fires here rise, and there descend,
> Explain his own beginning, or his end?[19]

which is, after all, as relating the world-within to the world-without, what concerns the poet. It is, however, in *The Dunciad*, that he scarifies the preposterous claims not, of course, of the really great scientist, but of scientism. The strength of his feeling that nature must be conceived of as organic, that the common feelings are what man lives by, raises hostility to the heights of great poetry. Listen to the Gloomy Clerk staking out his claim to the Goddess of Dulness:

> Let others creep by timid steps, and slow,
> On plain Experience lay foundations low,
> By common sense, to common knowledge bred,
> At last, to Nature's Cause thro' Nature led.

> All-seeing in thy mists, we want no guide,
> Mother of Arrogance, and Source of Pride!
> We nobly take the high Priori Road,
> And reason downward, till we doubt of God;
> Make Nature still incroach upon his plan;
> And shove him off as far as e'er we can:
> Thrust some Mechanic Cause into his place;
> Or bind in Matter, or diffuse in Space.
> Or, at one bound, o'erleaping all his laws,
> Make God Man's Image, Man the final Cause.[20]

Professor Marjorie Nicolson, however, has dealt so fully and beautifully with this phase, that I shall once more cast forward to the Romantics, other than Shelley.

Here we are faced by something far more fundamental to my general query. If the eighteenth century had suspected science because of its moral and metaphysical implications, now there makes its appearance the doubt, amounting to the very rejection, of a method which affected the whole operation of the human spirit. For by that time Newtonian physics had ceased to excite; they were too much taken for granted, and people's curiosity was being turned, as Wordsworth's remarks tend to show, to chemistry, botany, geology, and, we might add, the biological sciences. It was dawning upon men that science, far from making for a unified vision, such as the poet strives for, was, by its fragmentation of knowledge, making this more and more impossible. Had not Pope been right when he girded at those who

> See Nature in some partial narrow shape,
> And let the Author of the Whole escape.

and Wordsworth himself, not long after the encouraging Preface to *Lyrical Ballads*, asks in *The Prelude*:

> . . . who shall parcel out
> His intellect by geometric rules,
> Split like a province into round and square?

and, addressing Coleridge:

> Thou, my Friend! art one
> More deeply read in thy own thoughts; to thee
> Science appears but what in truth she is,
> Not as our glory and our absolute boast,
> But as a succedaneum, and a prop
> To our infirmity. No officious slave
> Art thou of that false secondary power
> By which we multiply distinction, then
> Deem that our puny boundaries are things
> That we perceive, and not that we have made.
> To thee, unblinded by these formal arts,
> The unity of all hath been revealed . . . [21]

Damning enough! But that is the philosopher. Here is the poet, protesting from the depths of his being, against the scientific approach:

> Nor should this, perchance,
> Pass unrecorded, that I still had loved
> The exercise and produce of a toil
> Than analytic industry to me
> More pleasing, and whose character I deem
> Is more poetic as resembling more
> Creative agency. The song would speak
> Of that interminable building rear'd
> By observation of affinities
> In objects where no brotherhood exists
> To passive minds . . .

It is the same attitude as in Blake's passionate outcry '. . . man has closed himself up till he sees all through narrow chinks of his cavern', or his saturnine

> May God us keep
> From single vision and Newton's sleep,[22]

though Blake, as we have seen, felt no inhibition against using a good deal of Newton for his imagery.

Yet many Romantics, at any rate when young, were intensely interested in science. They read widely, and exhibit a knowledge of at least Darwin's prose scientific studies as well as of his verse *Economy of Nature*. Coleridge, omnivorous reader, immersed himself in the dangerous element. He foregathered with, and wrote to Sir Humphrey Davy; he had read Newton's *Opticks*, and Priestley's, and was always dipping into the *Transactions of the Royal Society*: but he was quite prepared to put all these on a par with Burnet's gloriously fictional *Theory of the Earth*. What really excited him were all the curious things with which observant naturalists bejewelled the innumerable travel-books of his day. These things, as Livingstone Lowes put it, 'fecundated his imagination'.[23] He revelled in hearing of fishes, from which, as he transformed it, 'the elfish light Fell off in hoary flakes', and of phosphorescence generally, in knowing that 'slimy things' really did 'crawl with legs Upon the slimy sea'. It was nature as revealed to the ordinary eye that he cared for—like Akenside, not ungrateful to the scientist for pointing out the existence as well as the working out of things. At the same time he rebelled against the fragmentation of knowledge, or the partial generalisations which the scientific process entailed, as killing to the spirit; he even protested to Southey that the study of chemistry 'prevents, or tends to prevent, a young man from falling in love'. He enjoyed a good 'set-to' in its defence with such as Godwin, who attacked it ignorantly and dogmatically, but to Southey he revealed the depths of his mind:

> We all have obscure feelings, that must be connected with something or other—the miser with a guinea—Lord Nelson with a blue ribbon, Wordsworth's old Molly with her washing tub—Wordsworth with the hills, Lakes and trees (all men are poets in their way, tho' for the most part their ways are *damned bad ones*). Now chemistry makes a young man associate these feelings with inanimate objects—and that without any moral feeling of revulsion, but on the contrary with complete self-approbation, and his distant views of benevolence or his sense of immediate beneficences attach themselves either to man as the whole human race, or to man, as a sick man, as a painter, as a manu-

facturer, etc., and in no way to man as a husband, son, brother, daughter, wife, friend, etc., etc., . . . A young poet may do without being in love with a woman—it is enough if he loves—but to a young chemist it would be salvation to be downright romantically in love—and unfortunately so far from the poison and antidote growing together, they are like the wheat and the Barberry.[24]

Chemists, I believe, have been known to be in love; statistics are not available: but we can see what Coleridge was getting at. The study of a science, he found, canalises human responses, prevents the coming into being of the whole man, and therefore of the poet.

But why should we expect the Romantics, with their insistence on sensation, on the personality, on the creative power, to be lured by science? Everybody is familiar with Keats's furious rejection: 'philosophy' for him, would clip an angel's wings; it had put even the 'awful rainbow' 'in the dull catalogue of common things'. At Haydon's 'immortal dinner', he, Wordsworth and Lamb cheerfully drank Newton's health, but, as a happy corrective, 'confusion to mathematics'.

By the time the Victorian age got into its stride, scientism had been given a new twist. In the previous century the physicists and astronomers had altered man's views with respect to the nature of the universe, and their ideas had either become commonplace or flown off into the realms of philosophy. Now, at first, the work of the geologists altered man's view with regard to his place in the universe, and man, having got used to the vast enlargement of space, was now faced with the geologists' lengthening of time. It did not in itself become a poetic theme, though Tennyson absorbed it. Tennyson was immensely alive to the findings of scientists, though when scientists acclaimed him as a clever man, they were not seizing upon him as a scientist; they probably meant no more than to say that he must be intelligent because he did not raise up his hands in horror and cry 'This will never do!' He was,

indeed, clever, but in his poetry of scientism never got
much beyond the stage of telling, imaginatively enough,
what its findings were. When he wrote

> There where the long street roars, hath been
> The stillness of the central sea,[25]

he was simply picturing for the public what the geologists were saying. But he grasped the implications. Man
had become a mere passing trifle in a vast process, which
not only might modify his values, but which made nature
something quite regardless of him. 'Nature red in tooth
and claw' was utterly different from the old beneficent
milieu in which, for all its materialistic determinism, mankind had found a home. Tennyson, as a good public poet,
was sharpening the contemporary reaction to geological
discoveries when he cried:

> Are God and Nature then at strife
>   That Nature lends such evil dreams?
>   So careful of the type she seems,
> So careless of the single life; . . .

> 'So careful of the type?' but no
>   From scarped cliff and quarried stone
>   She cries, 'A thousand types are gone:
> I care for nothing, all shall go:'[26]

in a passage too well-known to need further quotation.

That was interesting enough, but not shocking. What
really disturbed men was what the biologists told them;
this radically altered man's conception of himself. Not that
the idea of evolution was new—it goes back to the Greeks,
and was familiar to the eighteenth century: but just as the
vastness of the universe made little impact on the imagination until its mechanism had been elucidated, so it was
not until *The Origin of Species* explained how evolution
worked, and revealed what might be the purpose, even the
motive spring of evolution, was there any profound reaction. Men had adjusted themselves easily enough to the

Newtonian universe, which had not after all made any change in the values by which they lived: but this might make a radical alteration. Yet the chief poets in the main left it alone, in spite of the fact that this scientific idea, which everybody could grasp, seemed at first sight to challenge the Christian concept of man's place in nature, indeed every old concept. If they did not ignore it altogether, or just show themselves aware of it, as Swinburne did in 'Hertha', they become poets of doubt. Meredith is the exception. He really made a poetic theme of it. Instead of treating it as the Newtonian poets had the revelation of their day, gone out and grasped it intellectually, he allowed it to act upon him till it became part of his intuition. Far from avoiding evolution, he translated it altogether out of the region of science, properly speaking. For him evolution was a series of steps from earth to mind, and thence to spirit: he could 'see in mould the rose unfold, the soul through blood and tears'. In 'Earth and Man' for instance, we read that

> On her great venture, Man
> Earth gazed while her fingers dint the breast
> Which is his well of strength, his home of rest,
> And fair to scan;

and he comforts man for the brutality of evolution: Earth

> . . . prompts him to rejoice,
> Yet scares him on the threshold with the shroud.
> He deems her cherishing of the best-endowed
> A wanton's choice.

There is nothing didactic, nothing descriptive about that. Meredith's is not scientific poetry, but the transformation of the universal law discovered by science into the kind of universal law that is, or may be, the poet's catalysing agent. He is carrying sensation, mental sensation at least, into the midst of the objects of science itself. So in 'The Woods of Westermain', in an exultant passage (after a reference to cattle ruminating 'back to hours when mind was mud'), man is called to look below the soul to earth, facing everything with enlightened courage:

> Then the reflex of that Fount
> Spied below, will Reason mount . . .
> Then your spirit will perceive
> Fleshly seeds of fleshly sins
> Where the passions interweave,
> How the serpent tangle spins
> Of the sense of earth misprised
> Brainlessly unrecognised;
> She being Spirit in her clods
> Footway to the God of Gods.
> Then for you are pleasures pure
> Sureties as the stars are sure . . .
> Pleasures that through blood run sane
> Quickening spirit from the brain.
> Each of each in sequent birth,
> Blood and brain and spirit, three
> (Say the deepest gnomes of Earth)
> Join for true felicity.

That, with its tremendous imagery, is transmuting science into something else; it is developing method into purpose; poetry is answering a question other than that posed by science.

To come to our own day. Can the poetic faculty free man from the limits with which scientism has circumscribed the internal world; or, to put it another way, light up the internal jungle it has created? If it is a question of fulfilling the need of the poet to universalise, the layman might think that nuclear physics ramifying into philosophy, and philosophy in turn ramifying into poetry, would serve. The limited generalisations of the theory of evolution, while making a dent, did not leave so lasting an impression on poetry as Newtonian physics did; thus it remains to be seen whether modern physics, if it can become scientism, and not infuriatingly snub us with mathematics, will stamp modern poetry.

For the moment, however, I will adventure into the fields of our two comparatively new, still perhaps groping sciences of anthropology and depth psychology. These— need one say it?—have alarmingly altered man's view of himself, the common man's. No one can ignore them, least of all the poet in so far as he retains his bardic function. Anthropology, however, was no prickly pear to swallow. When Frazer extended our historic threads into a mytho- logical past, and Jung revealed its persistence in our psyche—to the great service of Dr Edith Sitwell in the withering fisticuff satire of *Gold Coast Customs*—all this merely deepened our sense of tradition, of belonging, while linking up with our sense of relativity. It gave another dimension to *The Waste Land*. It revitalised myth, not as a classical reference or a tabloid generalisation, but as something which we live by now. As a public theme it has become indistinguishably merged in others.

Depth psychology was another matter; it shattered the old idea of personality as a stable core around which things build themselves up. The poet could not avoid it. We have already seen Mr Auden being used by it rather than allowing it to engender poetry: but later it became absor- bed into his intuitive imagination, as we see in *The Ascent of F6* and other work. There it illustrates a further stage, much more subtle, with numerous overtones making it, to instructed taste at least, far better poetry. But for a final stage I would turn elsewhere and take a passage from *The Dry Salvages*. I don't think Mr Eliot has ever directly touched depth-psychology—in *The Cocktail Party* he used it as a screen for something else, and not even as a symbol. But in *Four Quartets* generally it is part of a complex of themes, and is difficult to pick out because it is so fused with his general vision, especially of the nature of time.

> When the train starts, and the passengers are settled
> To fruit, periodicals, and business letters
> (And those who saw them off have left the platform)
> Their faces relax from grief into relief,

To the sleepy rhythm of a hundred hours.
Fare forward, travellers! not escaping from the past
Into different lives, or into any future;
You are not the same people who left that station
Or will arrive at any terminus,
While the narrowing rails slide together behind you;
And on the deck of the drumming liner
Watching the furrow that widens behind you . . .
At nightfall, in the rigging and the aerial,
Is a voice descanting (though not to the ear,
The murmuring shell of time, and not in any language)
'Fare forward, you who think you are voyaging;
You are not those who saw the harbour
Receding, or those who will disembark . . .'[27]

This partly treats of, is partly symbolic of, what is happening to the concept of self; but what depth psychology is in it—and there is far more than that in anything Mr Eliot may write—has been absorbed in the general imaginative vision, the universalisation.

Yet it cannot be said that since Shelley, with the possible exception of Meredith, scientism has in itself become a public theme. It is as though the poets soon realised with Coleridge and Wordsworth that unless it became so merged with the general consciousness as to be indistinguishable as science, it could not serve their purpose. It is certainly what has happened with Mr Eliot, if we can be sure it has happened there at all. But after all, the poet cannot ignore his fellow human beings, the scientists, if only because there are so many of them; and poets seem to be going back to a suggestion of Wordsworth's. He, it is significant, did not refer to the physicist, though he recognised chemistry as something likely to affect the impressions which we habitually receive. His impulses did not take him to the scientist's results, but to the man— what in soul *he* was. The botanist, so long as he does not peep and botanise upon his mother's grave, meets with his approval as a happy man:

H

The wandering Herbalist . . .
                              peeps round
For some rare floweret of the hill, or plant
Of craggy fountain; what he hopes for wins,
Or learns, at least, that 'tis not to be won . . .

Then, keen and eager, as a fine-nosed hound
By soul-engrossing instinct driven along
Through wood or open field, the harmless man
Departs, intent upon his onward quest.

His fellow-wanderer, the geologist, is not less to be envied;
he is almost as 'harmless', though his hammer makes some
scars

Beside our roads and pathways, though, thank Heaven!
This covert-nook reports not of his hand.

He has his felicities; he gathers a fragment, and

                         should crystal cube
Lurk in its cells, he thinks himself enriched,
Wealthier, and doubtless wiser, than before![28]

the exclamation mark exhibiting, it is to be feared, a certain scorn. And to-day, however much poets may feel that
they live in a different world from scientists, they feel also
that they are not altogether different animals. The two
may use language differently, see existence under such
opposed guises as hardly to be comprehensible to one
another, but after all they are both poor creatures that must
live. The poet therefore may properly be infinitely curious,
not so much as to what the scientist does, but as to what
kind of animal he is, what sort of mind he has. This in itself can be a poetic theme, or at least Mr MacNeice has
made it one in a section of his poem 'The Kingdom'.
Here, among others worthy of a place, is the scientist,
depicted with a sympathy based on understanding—the
understanding, it is assumed, of something alien, though
worthy of respect:

A little dapper man but with shiny elbows
And short keen sight, he lived by measuring things . . .
    . . . Obstinately
He canalised his fervour, it was slow
The task he set himself; but plotting points
On graph paper he felt the emerging curve
Like the first flutterings of an embryo
In somebody's first pregnancy; resembled
A pregnant man too in that his logic
Yet made the hidden child the centre of the world
And almost a messiah; so that here
Even over the shining test-tubes
The spirit of the alchemist still hovered
Hungry for magic, for the philosopher's stone . . .
    . . . Rules were rules
And all induction checked, but in the end
His reasoning hinged on faith and the first axiom
Was oracle or instinct . . .
His mind developed like an ancient church
By the accretion of side-aisles and the enlarging of lights
Till all the walls are windows and the sky
Comes in, if coloured; such a mind . . . a man . . .
Deserves a consecration; such a church
Bears in its lines the trademark of the Kingdom.[29]

That may be a little distant—the respectful salute of acquaintances passing in the street. But it is not patronising after the manner of Wordsworth. This attitude may become merged into a new sensibility towards which the scientist is perhaps leading us, and so become a public theme, and indeed Mr James Kirkup has gone a little further along the road; he does not stop at trying to realise what kind of man the scientist is, but enters into his emotions and actions, feeling with him as he does his job. In his startlingly actual 'A Correct Compassion' he makes a scientific finding shudderingly palpable. He addresses a surgeon performing a cardiac operation:

Cleanly, sir, you went to the core of the matter.
Using the purest kind of wit, a balance of belief and art,

> You with a curious nervous elegance laid bare
> The root of life, and put your finger on its beating heart.

As the poem proceeds an essential connection is made with ordinary human emotion, the imagination released beyond the actual scene. And the poem ends with the surgeon commenting:

> 'I should say that anatomically speaking
> This is a perfect case.—Anatomically.
>
> For of course, anatomy is not physiology.'
> We find we breathe again, and hear the surgeon hum.
> Outside, in the street, a car starts up. The heart regularly
> Thunders.—'I do not stitch up the pericardium.
>
> It is not necessary.'—For this is imagination's other place,
> Where only necessary things are done, with the supreme and
>   the grave
> Dexterity that ignores technique; with proper grace
> Informing a correct compassion, that performs its love, and
>   makes it live.[30]

This, with respect to scientism, may be imagination's other place, where its releasing power can inform the material the scientist supplies it with, as Shelley's did, we noticed, with what he received from Sir Humphrey Davy. It may provide a theme the general reader will respond to. It is no longer, obviously, a question of making the findings of science palpable to us as living and suffering beings —that is beyond the wildest imaginings—but to present them as a surrounding ethos. The findings escape even being trapped in the snare of the poetry of knowledge. When the layman reads of fabulously distant systems in the universe moving outward at a speed faster than light, his vision must be radically different from that of the mathematically trained scientist. What image can make that palpable? In chemistry it is much the same; there is no universalising alchemical approach, only diagrams of circles hung on to various arrangements of hooks. There are, indeed, the optimistic investigators of protein who hope

to discover what life is; but of these the layman is sceptical
—and even so the explained 'what' would only produce a
new 'why'. The idea of perpetual creation is exciting, and
Mr Heath-Stubbs gives us an example of how it may stir
the poet in his lines 'For the New Cosmology', as offered
to us by Mr Fred Hoyle:

> I saw the lady of galaxies at 12 a.m.
> Leaning over her cradles in a pallium of hydrogen.
> The Hyades in her hair, and the Seven Sisters,
> Orion crucified to the South, and the polar Bear,
> With the nebulae about her like whirling dervishes.
> 'Oh infinitely I aspire', she said, 'I am the ever-virgin
> And burning bush, created every minute
> By the miraculous seed in the vacancy of my loins;
> And cumbering my heart,
> Singing birds in a rage, an exaltation of nightingales.'[31]

But can the Great Directing Mind think of nothing
better than hydrogen? How can these things contribute
to a general state of being which would enable the poet
to make of them a great public theme? Can they be linked
up with the other assumptions upon which ordinary men
base their lives? If there are eternal truths which the scientist discovers, are they of any use for living; or for the
imagination when even the music of the spheres, we gather
from Sir Edward Appleton, is reduced to cosmic, or galac-
tic 'noises'? In his Eddington Memorial Lecture, Sir
Edmund Whittaker, following Whitehead, suggested that
the scientists' assurance to us that there are eternal verities
might form the basis of a kind of Stoicism; but when he
tells us in the same place that the great verity is Eddington's cosmic number we remain unmoved. Can we really
regard a number as a great creative principle behind some
process to which we should fit ourselves? Is 10^{78} among
the thoughts that voluntary move harmonious numbers?
You may, as he suggests, merge this with the Stoic notion
that the world process, subject to universal laws, is part of
God, or that God is the world process. A very desiccated

Stoicism: the world may end with a bang or a whimper. So that domains of science would not seem fruitful; they do no more than vaguely reinforce the religious intuition poets habitually use in public poetry.

Can more be hoped of other universal concepts? such perhaps as the notions that capture us when we, as laymen, bandy about the almost evocative phrase 'time-space continuum'; or when we are asked to conceive of existence made up of motion with no matter about it? Indeterminacy may give the imagination scope; at least it seems to the layman that here is something the scientist cannot measure: he will make about some phenomenon two contradictory statements which he declares are equally true. Are we here, perhaps, in a realm where science, philosophy and religion join hands? Is it possible for the creative power of the imagination to make out of these various scientific formulations some whole which the poet can communicate in poetry that will be generally read? Can he, in short, universalise? re-integrate the fragments? Mr Durrell finds the key to modern poetry in some such integration of man's apprehensions. Certainly our half-realised ideas of time as a pattern, rather than as a flow leading somewhere, seem to endow Mr Eliot with so strong an assurance as to provide the entrancing hypnotic music of *Four Quartets*.* If we respond it may be because it makes a link with the old archetypal image of Eternal Recurrence. As to our new conceptions of a fluid personality, the 'illusory self', are they too something we were acquainted with before, if only distantly? The idea dates back in our own era at least as far as Diderot, and we may have met it in Bradley: but, as with other 'discoveries', it did not strike the popular imagination until it was scientifically 'explained'. These notions may become general, and affect our attitudes. When they have permeated down, as items in the catalogue of common things, when they produce a general

* Mr Eliot on the whole scouts the importance of science: see *The Dry Salvages*, §V.

state, scientism may emerge as a great public theme. There
is already a sense of these notions. In common with Mr
Eliot, Mr Edwin Muir has the sense of time as a pattern,
but fuses it with his strong feeling of ancestral continuity,
making a more general appeal by relating it to local
patriotism. However, the time for that is not yet. For the
moment the most likely way for scientism to permeate
poetry would seem to be along the road first trodden by
Wordsworth.

CHAPTER V

PATRIOTISM I

O F all the obviously public themes, patriotism is the most obvious. Yet to embark upon discussing it awakes twinges of uneasiness, since patriotism has, as they would say in America, been smeared. It is true of course that it may figure as a cloak for the baser passions, or degenerate into the strident yelling of jingoism; it can be applied like a grease-paint to cover flagrant sins of the spirit. It was this false appearance that Mr Rex Warner jibed at when he wrote:

> You fat man!...
> Come with me if you can, and if not, go to hell
> with your comfy chairs, and your talk about the police,
> your doll wife, your cowardly life, your newspapers,
> your interests in the East,
> You, there, who are so patriotic, you liar, you beast![1]

For some it is intellectually hardly respectable. They feel with Martin Decoud in *Nostromo* that the word patriot has 'no sense for cultured minds, to whom the narrowness of every belief is odious'. But patriotism is not a belief. It is a basic assumption for living; or, as Ben Jonson put it: 'There is a necessity that all men should love their country: he that professeth the contrary may be delighted with his words, but his heart is there.'[2] In whatever way this love may make itself felt—as hope, or despair, or a vision—it has been a theme in poetry as early, shall we say, as Sophocles, or the Psalms, and it breaks through in an enormous amount of our own verse. We might even claim it to be among those 'inherited subjects', as Yeats put it, 'matter known to the whole people'—bardic themes, you may

say—with which I am here concerned. And such subjects
are interconnecting. Yeats went on to say:

> . . . I thought that in man and race alike there is something called
> 'Unity of Being', using that term as Dante used it when he com-
> pared beauty in the Convito to a perfectly proportioned human
> body. My father, from whom I learned the term, preferred a
> comparison to a musical instrument so strung, that if we touch a
> string all the strings murmur faintly.[3]

Patriotism might be called the sense of Unity of Being in
the population of a country. As a musical instrument it
has many strings: touch one, and others may vibrate or
jangle. And since Martin Decoud committed suicide,
having nothing spiritual to sustain him on his solitary
rock, we may recall the answer Antonia Avellanos made
him: 'The word you despise has stood also for sacrifice,
for courage, for constancy, for suffering.'

We cannot, of course, earmark those virtues for patriotism; they need not even belong to public themes; and I
would like to begin with a few suggestions as to some of
the poetry-making emotions we can call patriotic. For
this theme, being very complex, does not so clearly, so
undividedly, exhibit the same 'natural history' as the
others do—the didactic, the descriptive, the symbolic and
so on, though separate strands may. The emotions range
to heights of myth, from the homely, human, basically
social instinct that is felt as the love of the fellow-creatures
whom one knows; whose emotions, prejudices, vices, virtues and acts one understands, and perhaps forgives. It is
this patriotism we hear in such utterances as 'this land of
such dear souls, this dear, dear land', linking that love with
another patriotism, that of place. This further sentiment—
we are dealing with the poetry of sentiment—becomes
almost a mystic love of the soil from which you sprang, not
only because it holds the ashes of your fathers and the
temples of your gods, but because in it you have the roots
of your own being. It is as old as humanity, you might

think, one with the worship of the Earth Goddess. It is stated in very simple form by Kipling in one of his most nursery-hymn metres, exemplifying so late in the day the didactic phase:

> God gave men all the earth to love,
> But since our hearts are small,
> Ordained for each one spot should prove
> Beloved over all.[4]

It is, I imagine, to this sense that we ordinarily give the name of patriotism. Halifax expressed it in a famous passage:

> But for the Earth of England, tho perhaps inferior to that of many places abroad, to him [the Trimmer] there is Divinity in it, and he would rather dye than see a spike of *English* grass trampled down by a foreign trespasser.[5]

It is only a short step from this to a third sense, that of one's country as the vehicle of a tradition, an embodiment of it, issuing as a personification. 'Methinks I see in my mind a noble and puissant nation, rousing herself like a strong man after sleep, and shaking her invincible locks.'[6]

These on the whole have been the main chords; but the instrument has undergone various re-tunings, and like the other themes, has had many strings added to it. Each of those I have mentioned has certainly in its most obvious simplicity proved metre-making, not least in the drama. It doesn't follow that what a dramatist puts in the mouth of his character is what he himself feels, but at least he will use what he knows he can depend upon to evoke an immediate response. There is more than a little of what we to-day look upon as vulgar jingoism even in Shakespeare—such words as 'For England never did nor ever shall Lie at the proud foot of a conqueror', and all the vaunting speeches in *Henry V*. For deeper feelings we must go to *Richard II*, and I would add the phrase 'this happy breed of men' to those I have already quoted from that play, for that is the string I would like to touch first.

Its vibrations are not always very pleasant to our ears; there was a little too much of schoolboy bragging about it in the early days when the nationalistic idea was coming into being, such as an Englishman being worth ten Frenchmen, as we find in Drayton's *Ballad of Agincourt*, an unduly popular poem. Is it, we may ask, popular precisely because it does express latent feelings few of us would admit to sharing—at any rate in so crude a form? But together with that, Drayton gives us, with didactic directness, the sense of fellowship with one's countrymen which is at the root of a good deal of patriotism:

> None from his fellow starts,
> But playing manly parts
> And like true English hearts
>   Stuck close together:

as though the sense of community were the important thing, Burke's love of the little platoon. And we remember from our boyhood days—since the lines were to be found in any child's anthology—that Scott's 'wretch' who never to himself had said 'This is my own, my native land', was 'concentred all on self'. The feeling persists, if only as an underlying theme, even among the wrenchings and striations of modern political emotion. Mr Auden, in the full tide of his earlier international idealism, recognised the drag a sense of his country may have on a man, the longing for the union of *its* people: in its complexity it is mixed with place-patriotism.

> Look what we stand on, the bone-rich soil of England;
> It has thrust us together, it is stronger than we.
> In it our separate sorrows are a single hope,
>   It's in its nature always to appear
>   Behind us as we move
>   With linked arms through our dreams,
>   Wherefore apart we love
>   Its sundering streams.[7]

and he refers to 'the millions who wish to be one'.

But you cannot love people by the million—unless indeed you're a bureaucrat; and the poetry of sentiment cannot reach great intensity with such vague blanket ideas: it must deal with specific actualities, as fact or symbol. Thus Yeats, voicing his love of the Irish, is precise. Normally his inner necessity, his magnificent pride, turns him to the great patriots, his poetry being shot with the names of Emmet and others, particularly that of Parnell; yet there was something in the spirit of the humble too, that moved him to song, an epic quality perhaps in their tradition as an aristocracy of servers:

> Irish poets, learn your trade,
> Sing whatever is well made,
> Scorn the sort now growing up
> All out of shape from toe to top,
> Their unremembering hearts and heads
> Base-born products of base beds.
> Sing the peasantry , and then,
> Hard-riding country gentlemen,
> The holiness of monks, and after
> Porter-drinkers' randy laughter;
> Sing the lords and ladies gay
> That were beaten into the clay
> Through seven heroic centuries;
> Cast your mind on other days
> That we in coming days may be
> Still the indomitable Irishry.[8]

That, you may say, is mere affectionate cataloguing; but in the poetry of sentiment, sentiment is after all the main ingredient; the poetry tends to be simple and direct. By its nature, as opposed to the poetry of passion, it demands statement rather than imagery.

To touch that string sets others vibrating. For if, with Wordsworth, you regard patriotism 'as a specialised or concentrated form of the love of mankind', to quote Miss Helen Darbishire; and if, as he did, you hold soldiership to be the issue of moral virtue, several strings will hum

together. The soldier brings to a focus, makes actual, the
vague notion implicit in the phrase 'this land of such dear
souls'. But now, with him, the primitive sentiment is
pierced through by the more conscious intellection, and
the soldier or sailor becomes a symbol. It was so with
Collins when he wrote the poem beginning

> How sleep the Brave, who sink to Rest
> By all their Country's Wishes blest!

Here then we have something which adds a late complexity to the theme. Its apparent simplicity makes it a
readily public one, yet it is a deceptive simplicity, because
the soldier or sailor is quite unwittingly symbolic. Mr
Hamish Henderson puts it plainly enough in *Elegies for
the Dead in Cyrenaica* ('End of a Campaign'):

> There were our own, there were the others.
> Their deaths were like their lives, human and animal.
> There were no gods, and precious few heroes.
> What they regretted when they died had nothing to do with race
>   and leader, realm indivisible,
> laboured Augustan speech or vague imperial heritage
> (They saw through that guff before the axe fell).

Guff perhaps; but there was something more instinctive.
As Mr Roy Campbell makes his 1st N.C.O. say in the
'Jungle Eclogue' in *Talking Bronco*:

> One's faith, together with one's native land,
> Beyond all ideologies must stand.

Statement, however, though it might have been enough
for public poetry at the time of *The Ballad of Agincourt*, cannot much serve the poet once the theme has developed
beyond a primitive stage. The theme may, however,
mingle with a wider one, even though patriotism is not
the poet's accustomed realm of being, even seldom visited,
and it may come at a high level of intensity. It did with
Gerard Hopkins in:

> Yes. Whý do we áll, seéing of a soldier bless him? bless
> Our redcoats, our tars? Both being, the greater part,
> But frail clay, but foul clay. Here it is: the heart
> Since, proud, it calls the calling manly, gives a guess
> That, hopes that, makes believe, the men must be no less.

That extremely packed passage invites more than the salutation of animal bravery: it asks the reader to feel bound to respect courage that subsists for the sake of an idea, dimly realised by the man himself, but profoundly felt by the poet. His heart sees 'some where, some man do all that man can do for love'.

But I will go back to Yeats's poem. There we may have caught a note often heard, another string that is almost a main one. It is the fear that the men of to-day are not what their fathers were, a note which has from the first sounded persistently in English poetry. It is one of reproach, and helps to establish tradition as a main sentiment in patriotism. This at once makes the music far more contrapuntal, since the sense of tradition is itself complex. And it is this which constitutes the appeal in the reproachful passages, essentially public utterances, since they are meant to be heard so as to induce 'unity of being'. How much the general reader responds is made plain by so many such passages being among the best known in the language. Who is not familiar with Cowper's deeply felt, splendidly rhythmed

> England, with all thy faults I love thee still—
> My country! and, while yet a nook is left
> Where English minds and manners may be found
> Shall be constrain'd to love thee . . . ?[9]

This does not yet demand very complex poetry; it is descriptive, and with Cowper it involves imagery only when he comes to speak of 'the ark' of England's 'magnificent and awful cause', which invites other themes. In that passage as a whole there are ten strings that murmur. But patriotism here requires more than simple praise, since

this note administers a moral medicine. It links up with
Stoicism when Cowper speaks with scorn of the effemi-
nates who love when they should fight. And if it is among
the functions of poetry to express the common sense of
what man ought to be, not only with respect to the gods,
but also with respect to his fellows, reproachful patriotism
has served it well as a symbol. What must be one of Wordsworth's most widespread sonnets will illustrate its assured
potency. Thousands must have got off by heart:

> Milton! thou should'st be living at this hour:
> England hath need of thee. She is a fen
> Of stagnant waters: altar, sword and pen,
> Fireside, the heroic wealth of hall and bower,
> Have forfeited their ancient English dower
> Of inward happiness. We are selfish men . . .

the octet ending with a mixed invocation, that I would ask
you to remember later, that we should be given 'manners,
virtue, *freedom*, power'.

There is a good strong scent of nostalgia about the
reproachful passages. Nostalgic to-day is a pejorative
epithet, as though it were wrong to remember, to look
back, and to love: but it forms part of a good deal of the
life of sentiment, and is the basis of not a little excellent
poetry. The passages recall a visionary past, the theme of
a departed Golden Age which for some time haunted the
thoughts of men. But they need not always contain this
sentiment; they may be sheer scolding. Sylvester, at the
early end of my bracket, used it for a vigorous all-round
scarification of what might certainly be

> . . . (deere ALBION) Europe's Pearle of Price,
> The World's rich garden, Earth's rare Paradice

but was also 'wanton England'.

> Thy uncontroll'd, bold, open Atheism: [he scourges]
> Close Idol-service: cloaked hypocrism . . .
> Wealth's mercy-less *Wrong*, *Usury*, *Extortion*:
> Poore's *Idleness*, *repining* at thir portion:

> Thy *Drunken Surfets*; and *Excesse* in *Diet*:
> Thy *Sensuall* wallowing in *Lascivious Riot*:
> Thy huff'd, puff'd, painted, curl'd, purl'd, *wanton Pride* . . .[10]

and a good deal more. But there, one feels, Sylvester is simply hugely enjoying himself rather than being serious, indulging in the heady vituperation of all vice, fashionable in his day, if only to prove that the sect you belonged to was as morally sound as the other man's. At the other end there is Kipling's scornful denunciation, this time deadly serious, in 'No doubt but ye are the people', a people childishly unforeseeing, unwilling to pay the price for safety, contenting their souls 'With flannelled fools at the wicket or the muddied oafs at the goals'. The catalogue is as long as Sylvester's, but the moral is really pointed, exact, while the sins, sloth and sensuality, are more subtle, the people being

> Arid, aloof, incurious, unthinking, unthanking, gelt—

clothed in all the sterile vices that are the prey of every satirist. There is no looking back there, no hankering after a vanished past, but a vivid realisation of the present. The superstructure we see, from the first is varied, for reproach as a public theme involves men as an organised community, itself a complex idea dovetailed with the sense of tradition, of something that has been created.

Yet it usually comes out in plain straightforward verse; this sentiment, we realise, is less profound, more easily rationalised, than the love of the earth which has always been part of most of us. This almost mystic sense demands more figurative expression. Thus, for John of Gaunt in *Richard II* his country is, as with Sylvester, a jewel:

> This precious stone, set in a silver sea . . .
> This blessed plot, this earth, this realm, this England,

the whole passage exhibiting, as Signor Leone Vivante says in his judgments of English poetry, 'a lightning-like transparency, revealing a reality (a reality of thought)

which [does] not exist generally in mere contemplation'.
That is, it is not a private thought; it is a shared emotion,
which Bolingbroke too uttered as he went off to exile:

> Then England's ground, farewell; sweet soil adieu:
> My mother, and my nurse, that bears me yet!

expressing the profound sense of soil echoed by Richard
when he comes back from Ireland:

> I weep for joy
> To stand upon my kingdom once again.
> Dear earth, I do salute thee with my hand.

Shakespeare, it may be, was deliberately helping to affirm
this sentiment, which, at least until we stiffened into
urbanisation, must have been felt, however obscurely, by
most people. For everyone in the play is not so whole-
hearted. The Bishop of Carlisle, when reporting the death
of Norfolk in Italy, remarks that he

> at Venice gave
> His body to that pleasant country's earth,

Italy being the paradise of Renaissance man. Drayton also
seems to have felt the need for affirmation. As author of
Polyolbion, that vast compendium of England's delights,
with its songs in praise of England's flowers, he would have
none of this fashionable sophistication. His Earl of Surrey
in the Heroicall Epistle to the Lady Geraldine would have
been at odds with the Bishop. 'I find no cause', he declares,

> nor judge I reason why
> My country should give place to *Lumbardy*.
> As goodly flowers on *Thamesis* doe growe
> As beautify the Bankes of wanton *Po*;
> As many Nymphs as haunt rich *Arnus* strand
> By silver *Severne* tripping hand in hand.

Sylvester is more confident. In translating Du Bartas he
will on no account have England left out. Is France in any
way better than England? Perish the thought! So when-

I

ever his French author praises something French, Sylvester counters with an English example. And just as the denizens of the sea, sturgeons and lampreys, 'who needs will home', and 'in the ireful Ocean go to seek their Tomb', so

> ... English Gallants that in Youth do go
> To visit *Rhine, Sein, Ister, Arn,* and *Po;*
> Where though their Sense be dandl'd, dayes and nights,
> In sweetest choice of changeable Delights,
> They never can forget their Mother-Soyl,
> But hourly home their hearts and eyes recoyl,
> Long languishing with an extream Desire
> To see the smoak of their dear Native Fire.[11]

a sentiment echoed by Macaulay when his exiled Jacobite

> Heard on Lavernia Scargill's whispering trees,
> And pined by Arno for [his] lovelier Tees.[12]

How can the poet normally express, except nakedly, this profound, primitive feeling? It would seem to call for simplicity, if it is to be a public theme, phrased with all the power that simplicity demands. Shakespeare alone seems to have been able to raise it above the didactic level, to fuse it with actual living, to bring it to such passionate heights as to make imagery imperative.

The sense nevertheless is always with us, and is what Rupert Brooke was trying to express in the sonnet, too readily derided and hurriedly classified as 'sentimental' (perhaps because it is too often iambically mouthed out)

> If I should die, think only this of me,
> That there's some corner of a foreign field
> That is for ever England . . .[13]

Again I would point out that this is the poetry people read. But the feeling soon merges into something else, into a passion of the countryside as one knows it in all its loved familiarity and associations, leading to such a cry as 'Oh, to be in England, now that April's there!' This is apt to

drop into passages not much more than descriptive, such
as Drayton supplied, and John Phillips was to offer his
readers some hundred years later in *Cider*. Such 'impulses'
also are always present, and we have them again in Cowper
in the paragraph of which I quoted a part, and which takes
us back to Drayton's contention: however much England's
clime

> Be fickle, and [the] year, most part deform'd
> With dripping rains, or wither'd by a frost

nothing would induce him to exchange the sullen skies
for the vines of France or Ausonia's golden fruitage and
her myrtle bowers.

The poet can always be sure of being read if he touches
upon this theme, or at least could till quite lately. It was by
so doing that he imparted his patriotism at the beginning
of the 1914 war, accompanying it with the expression of a
deep sense that it was all worth paying for, even with life.
Robert Nichols, for instance, in 'At the Wars':

> O yellow-hammer, once I heard
> Thy yaffle, when no other bird
> Could to my sunk heart comfort bring;
> So sharp thy note is with the pain
> Of England I may not see again!
> Yet sing thy song: there answereth
> Deep in me a voice that saith:
> *The gorse upon the twilit down,*
> *The English loam so sunset brown,*
> *The bowed pines and the sheep-bell's clamour,*
> *The wet, lit lane, and the yellow-hammer,*
> *The orchard and the chaffinch song*
> *Only to the Brave belong,*
> *And he shall lose that joy for aye*
> *If their price he cannot pay,*
> *Who shall find them dearer far*
> *Enriched by blood after long war.*[14]

In much the same way, Mr Ivor Gurney, after speaking of the secret beauty miraculously shining in the landscape of England, ended his poem with:

> Think on me too, O Mother, who wrest my soul to serve you
> In strange and fearful ways beyond your encircling waters:
> None but you can know my heart, its tears and sacrifice
> None, but you, repay.[15]

The impulse behind these poems is, evidently, self-dedication to familiar things.

We do not, however, merely receive poems; we go on to ask ourselves questions about the poems we read, not always consciously, but as part of the sifting process by which we determine value. It is not enough just to have our own feelings reflected back to us; we must experience them at an acuter level of awareness. We ask, 'How far does this illumine life?' For that, after all, is what the poet is, or ought to be, doing for us. He is not merely reacting to a net of circumstance in which he finds himself caught, at least not reacting without the cogitation, conscious or subconscious, which makes the poem into something more than the record of a person-thing relation. The question comes: 'Is what is said of importance to me; or, with a public theme, to all of us?' What can too easily happen in poetry of this sort is that the poet is doing no more than remind us of sentiments we share; he can rely on a stock response. Not that the stock response need be meaningless: there may even be some virtue in it. Perhaps it is because the poets of to-day so sedulously fight shy of it that they do not get the readers that they might. There is no need for all poetry to be disturbing; it is enough, at least in the realms I am discussing, that it should revive, or reaffirm, some of the assumptions by which we live. It is to this category that most of the poems I have quoted belong. By their nature they have little of that concentration which we perhaps too mechanically demand, since they depend upon a series of recollected moments; there is no

new revelation. Therefore imagery of any symbolic kind
is rare; it seems to occur only with very great poets, as in
John of Gaunt's speeches in *Richard II*, part of which I
reminded you of, and to which Ivor Gurney's 'encircling
waters' may be a reference.

Moreover, dedication to a thing, or to a set of physical
experiences, is by itself an impossibility. So, as with much
of the scientific poetry I touched upon, nature description
—for this is what this sort of patriotic poetry largely
amounts to—is itself a symbol for something within. It is
what these things stand for that causes poetic pressure.
And what they stand for here is a tradition in which spiritual human experience has a formative part. In addition
to the instinctive love of the soil, of the native haunt, of the
lie of the land, and of its people, for great poetry there has
to be, it would seem, some generally felt directive idea.
It need not necessarily be something reasoned, but it must
be something that can be reasoned about. To be justified,
it must be more than what is almost an animal instinct.
It has to create a vision which embraces more than the
immediate community, something that the imagination
can act upon. It involves, indeed, the mythopeic power;
and in England a myth, with common feeling as its basis,
was created or given shining life by the poets. It became
a public theme.

It begins, as I see it, with Shakespeare, and in view of
where he stands historically, it is not to be wondered at
that it should be based on the myth of royalty. In royalty,
to help us make up a more inclusive theme, we have
another primitive, intuitive sense which we have been consciously aware of ever since we read *The Golden Bough*.
We are to-day familiar with the idea of the mystic bond
believed by primitive tribes to exist between the health of
their ruler and their own welfare. How far this remains
part of the collective subconscious it would be hard to say.
Our present patriotism is dependent on some three hundred years of history, and is riddled with doubts: like

other values it has had to be hammered out under the stress of living. Yet it is notable that whenever one of our sovereigns dies, millions are profoundly moved. There comes upon them, however triflingly and fleetingly, a sense of calamity. Mr G. M. Trevelyan, indeed, speaks of the inviolable bonds between king and subject as an instinct

> born in every child of the race .. wrapped up in a thousand mysterious associations with a remote and still unbroken past, transmitted from father to son through thirty generations.[16]

In Elizabethan times, it is fairly safe to say, the mystique of royalty was hardly to be distinguished from that of country, as anyone may see by reading through the 'Astrœa' sequence of Sir John Davies; but its richest expression comes, as we might expect, from Shakespeare. John of Gaunt touches upon it in the phrases 'this sceptred isle'—'this teeming womb of royal kings', but it comes out in full in the prophetic speech Cranmer makes over the babe Elizabeth at the end of *Henry VIII*. I must make rather long extracts, because so much is conveyed, so many strings made to vibrate.

> This royal infant—Heaven still move about her!—
> Though in her cradle, yet now promises
> Upon this land a thousand thousand blessings,
> Which time shall bring to ripeness . . .
>   Saba was never
> More covetous of wisdom and fair virtue
> Than this pure soul shall be: . . .
>   . . . her own shall bless her;
> Her foes shall shake like a field of beaten corn,
> And hang their heads with sorrow: good grows with her.
> In her days every man shall eat in safety
> Under his own vine what he plants; and sing
> The merry songs of peace to all his neighbours . . .
> Nor shall this peace sleep with her: but as when
> The bird of wonder dies, the maiden phoenix,
> Her ashes new create another heir
> As great in admiration as herself:

So she shall leave her blessedness to one . . .
Who from the sacred ashes of her honour
Shall star-like rise, as great in fame as she was,
And so stand fixed. Peace, plenty, love, truth, terror,
That were the servants to this chosen infant
Shall then be his, and like a vine grow to him:

and here the prophetic part, from which the myth grew:

Wherever the bright sun in heaven shall shine,
His honour and the greatness of his name
Shall be, and make new nations.

A vision of what might be, a golden age, not in the past, but in the future. The conception is organic, it grows from its roots: it is plastic, and can be moulded by the poetic imagination. And it is from about this time, I venture, that began that myth—and a myth is nothing if not a public theme—which was to persist for some three or four generations, to be modified as the years went on, but always to engender poetry.

It was now, perhaps, that the idea of England as a symbol first came into being. Naturally, we might think; for here was a country just realising itself. It had repelled a formidable invader; it was making discoveries in the West, feeling all the excitement of adventure, of power, of expansion. But to what end? What were the glorious exploits of the Drakes and Frobishers and Raleighs for? Man—at least civilised man—cannot live by rapacity alone. Peace, plenty, love, truth, terror, and new nations arising; what is the poetic mind, interpreting and moulding that of the averagely imaginative man, to do with all this? Shakespeare's tremendous, and generally appealing vision, was put into popular non-dramatic form, waveringly, not very long after, in a poem commonly read for some two hundred years, Denham's *Cooper's Hill*. This is far more than a 'place' poem. It is a historical conspectus, and something of a philosophic poem; it has more than a little to do with the assumptions by which men live. Here I am thinking

especially of the passage about the Thames, which ends
with the famous quatrain that I shall spare you. It runs:

> But godlike his unweary'd bounty flows;
> First loves to do, then loves the good he does.
> Nor are his blessings to his bank confined,
> But free and common, as the sea or wind:
> When he to boast, or to disperse his stores
> Full of the tribute of his grateful shores
> Visits the world, and in his flying tow'rs
> Brings home to us, and makes the Indies ours;
> Finds wealth where 'tis, bestows it where it wants,
> Cities in desarts, woods in cities plants.
> So that to us, no thing, no place is strange,
> While his fair bosom is the world's exchange.

There you get the dream of the world as one unified
polity, even if unified by British commerce, a vision which
is still ours, though now very hesitantly. England is to be,
not so much the agent, as the vehicle of a strange transformation, and it was this concept that came to move to
great utterance the two most considerable poets of the
Augustan era. Dryden developed it, and gave it form, at
the end of *Annus Mirabilis*, when speaking of London after
the Great Fire:

> Methinks already from this Chymick flame,
> I see a city of more precious mould:
> Rich as the town, which gives the Indies name,
> With Silver paved, and all divine with Gold.

It is worth looking at those lines. Dryden, we see, is using
alchemical imagery; it is not the gold of the counting-
house he is talking about, but that produced by chymick
fire; the town which gave the Indies name is Mexico, and
he is describing, not a world market, but the New Jeru-
salem.

> More great than human now, and more *August*,

(the use of the capital letter and italics for 'august' show
that he is punning on London's old name of Augusta)

> Now deified, she from her Fires does rise:
> Now widening Streets on new Foundations trust,
> And, opening, into larger parts she flies,

the 'ambiguous' phoenix imagery being perhaps a reference to Cranmer's speech. The whole quatrain is symbolical; the new foundations are not crude bricks and mortar. And as the poem draws to its conclusion, the vision becomes, though not consistently so, less and less factual:

> ... she will behold
> From her high Turrets, hourly Sutors come:
> The East with Incense, and the West with Gold,
> Will stand, like Suppliants, to receive her doom.

The final stanza takes shape in entirely new imagery:

> Thus to the Eastern wealth through Storms we go,
> But now, the Cape once doubled, fear no more:
> A constant Trade-wind will securely blow,
> And gently lay us on the spicy shore.

It is not a vision of power or conquest; it has nothing, as *we* would use the word, imperialistic about it. The theme is public enough, vitalised by the poetic imagination, become symbol. It was so with Pope when he took it up, combining Denham with Dryden, and adding something of his own, a string that was to vibrate very loudly. It comes in the long prophetic part uttered by Thames which virtually concludes *Windsor Forest*. I abstract a few lines:

> The time shall come, when free as sea or wind
> Unbounded *Thames* shall flow for all mankind,
> Whole nations enter with each swelling tyde,
> And Seas but join the regions they divide;
> Earth's distant ends our glory shall behold,
> And the new world launch forth to meet the old ...
> Oh stretch thy reign, fair Peace! from shore to shore,
> Till conquest cease, and slav'ry be no more;
> Till the freed Indians in their native groves
> Reap their own fruits, and wooe their sable Loves,
> *Peru* once more a race of Kings behold,
> And other *Mexico's* be roof'd with gold.

And we see that by now something has happened to the theme; it has developed, as did those of Stoicism and Scientism, from something simple, didactic almost, in a sense personal, to the stage of bearing a complex super-structure, expressible not as statement, but in imagery. Even in the small extract I have read, this is tremendously varied and suggestive, crammed with references. Alche-mical gold is there, the symbolical Mexico, the man who shall eat in safety under his own vine what he planted. The theme, claiming its publicity as part of a peace-poem meant to be widely read, was never more richly sounded, many chords vibrating simultaneously. An important new one was added: 'and slav'ry be no more'. But the main theme was gradually to disentangle itself from a number of accretions before becoming something else.

As we have seen, the early eighteenth century was a bumper age for public themes, and it developed what was dubbed a 'rage for patriotism'. It was not a theme the poets were afraid to tackle, feeling with Shaftesbury that 'Of all human Affections, the noblest and most becoming human Nature, is that of LOVE to one's Country', but I must excuse myself from going into it fully here as I have treated of it elsewhere.[17] I will limit myself to distinguish-ing one or two strings, for the poets were to find the myth pierced by a new doctrine. There was in the air an excited feeling of expansion, not now, as in Elizabethan times, of human enlargement into worlds unknown, but of mercan-tilism. Not a very pretty subject, one would think, nor very nourishing to the human imagination. Yet there it was, very much in the hearts of Englishmen—a cursory reading of Defoe will prove that—and the poets, from Prior in *Carmen Seculare* (1700) to Dyer in *The Fleece* (1756) were doing no more than express their age, re-sponding to the need of men to have the emotions by which they lived clarified for them in verse. But that sort of emo-tion does not rank as one of the basic assumptions by which men most fully live. It may be a public theme, but not a

poetic public one, since it does not give the formative
imagination enough to do. 'Peaceful commerce from divi-
dable shores' is all very well, but Ulysses lumped it with
degrees in schools and the prerogative of age—not metre-
making subjects. What the poets did was to make commerce into a symbol which would form part of the myth.
For Edward Young, commerce gave arts as well as gain;
for Fenton it made the arts survive; according to Savage
it encouraged public works, and for Glover it charmed
helpless man, forlorn and wild, to 'sweet society'. In short
it was the great civilising agency which bountiful Thames
was to spread over the whole world. The theme is thicken-
ing; all sorts of responses are being demanded of the
reader. It is engendering complex poetry, which does not
however rise to much tension; it is on the whole poetry of
descriptive statement, as in *The Fleece*, which becomes a
patriotic poem through glorifying the wool trade. Yet
Dyer made a further contribution to the myth—by which,
incidentally we still to some extent live. After disclaiming
arms, as being useless to an island, he goes on:

> She [England] ne'er breaks
> Her solemn compacts, in the lust of rule:
> Studious of arts and trade, she ne'er disturbs
> The holy peace of states. 'Tis her delight
> To fold the world with harmony . . .[18]

The *pax Britannica* has come into being. But the word harmony is worth noting; it is relating the theme to something far more universal: another dimension is being
added.

And at this time a further idea seized powerfully upon
the popular imagination as something very vital to living;
that of freedom. Pope suggested its larger implications,
but at this period a great deal of it was purely factious.
The words 'patriot' and 'patriotism' became largely party
parrot cries, used against Walpole, who for the disap-
pointed opposition was the bugbear, the oppressor, the

tyrannic smotherer of liberty. Much of the clamour was absurd, and as Berkeley said, 'Being loud or vehement either against a court or for a court, is no proof of patriotism':[19] but much of it corresponded with the sense, very real at the time, that freedom was a precious possession that had only lately been won, and wasn't by any means secure. The myth then became enriched by the idea that persists to-day, that England was not only, as men and women still sing, the land of hope and glory, but also the mother of the free. Whence Thomson's poem *Liberty*, which though already in Dr Johnson's time consigned to the shelf to harbour dust and spiders, and perhaps not very much read when fresh from the press, represented enormous labour on Thomson's part. No mere dithyramb, but a compendious history of civilisation, it is built up on the axiom that wherever civilisation exists there the goddess Liberty has her abode. She had alighted first in Greece, flitted to Rome, appeared in more modern Italy (the form is met again in Shelley's 'Ode to Liberty') and had finally come to settle in England. (Tennyson repeats the idea in 'Of Old Sat Freedom'.) There is no doubt, not only that Thomson (among other poets) felt this profoundly, but that he was writing typically public poetry when he made the goddess refer to Britain as

> . . . my best-established, last,
> And, more than Greece or Rome, my steady reign;

Only where liberty is monarch can the arts flourish. It is a dreary poem; the pressure hardly ever rises to poetic strength, and most readers preferred his more succinct statement at the end of 'Rule Britannia', where he sang that

> The Muses, still with freedom found
> Shall to thy happy coast repair.

Then, as a further accretion to the myth, there came into being a sub-theme frequent enough in future poetic utterance, that England was the refuge of the oppressed. It is

still part of the myth. The England of that date was familiar enough with refugees, especially in the form of Hugue-
nots, and as early as 1715 Croxall in *The Vision* rhymed
of the scene in the spacious shade of St Paul's, where you
could

> From foreign climes see injur'd people come,
> Invoking Aid beneath its ample Dome;
> And hospitably form a safe Retreat
> From the fierce Flames of persecuting Heat.

Dyer echoed the sentiment, and so, a little less hospitably
did Thomson: he felt there was more room in the colonies
for 'those whom bigots chase from foreign lands'.

His very lukewarmness suggests this did not at that
time appeal very deeply to sentiment; and it is, after all,
the poetry of sentiment that we are here dealing with. But
what now filtered in to add to the primitive blood-feeling
was a theme congruous with the growing historic sense of
the age—the contribution of Britain to the roll of world-
famous men. It had begun earlier; but Denham, and later
Pope and a number of lesser fry (Diaper, John Phillips
and others) tended to confine themselves to great mon-
archs. Nevertheless the idea had begun to become more
specific with Dryden. In the 'Epistle to Dr Charleton',
which I referred to in a previous chapter, after heaving his
sigh of relief at the release of the human spirit from the
tyrannic rule of Aristotelian reason, he goes on:

> Among th' Assertor's of free Reason's claim
> Th' English are not the least in Worth, or Fame,

and proceeds with his record of scientists. In the eighteenth
century that of Newton could be proudly added, but
Thomson in *Summer* included many other groups, notably
the 'assertors' of political freedom, such as Milton and
Harrington, and then the great poets. The notion stirs the
fibres of everyone who has a sense of tradition; it involves
pride, as well as the humble thought that we are no better
than our fathers. It is a sentiment that gains immediate

response: Let us all praise famous men, and their fathers
that begot them—and also in some measure begot us. The
poetry proper to this Collingwood called 'magic', as meant
to lead to action, or at least an attitude of mind, and some
of it we cherish. We all know, for instance, that sonnet of
Wordsworth's in the series 'Dedicated to Liberty':

> Great men have been among us; hands that penn'd
> And tongues that uttered wisdom—better none:
> The later Sydney, Marvel, Harrington,
> Young Vane and others who call'd Milton Friend.

Here, we see, there is a change. These were not men of
great political power or scientific eminence: they were
great for another reason:

> These moralists could act and comprehend:
> They knew how genuine glory was put on;
> Taught us how rightfully a nation shone
> In splendour: what strength was that would not bend
> But in magnanimous meekness . . .

Again, with a new theme, didactic poetry of statement,
with only the barest, most commonplace imagery. When
grown older, as with Yeats, it becomes symbolic:

> I declare this tower is my symbol; I declare
> This winding, gyring, spiring treadmill of my
>   stair is my ancestral stair;
> That Goldsmith, and the Dean, Berkeley and Burke
>   have travelled there.[20]

But with him the note tends, perhaps, to the personal. Yet
if it is not altogether a public utterance, it echoes a popular feeling. It has nothing to do with the private struggles
which engender poetry of the highest tension.

But at all events we can see that the simple public theme
has become almost unrecognisably transformed. The plain
love of the soil has been made to carry an extremely varied
superstructure. It has grown to an acknowledgment of a
national tradition. And though it may ever and anon come

back to a purely instinctive basis, it then becomes intellectualised, justified, made much more complex. It is no longer simply the poetry of sentiment. It implies, besides love, responsibility, a historic sense. The myth again is no longer a Utopian vision, but something far more suited to adults; it involves experience, of history and of men. It therefore engages poets in a quite different way. It cannot be, or need not be, lyrically sung. For its full expression, description alone is not enough, and its tends to be implicit, not directly stated: for the country of a man's birth has become a symbol, not only of his deepest biological feelings, but of important human values, threshed out by time. And what is further interesting about this theme is that it develops into something else.

CHAPTER VI

PATRIOTISM II

AT the end of my last chapter, I suggested that patriotic poetry underwent an evolution which brought it to express a highly complex group of feelings or intuitions; it could no longer be regarded merely as the poetry of sentiment. This state of affairs does not necessarily result in symbolism, nor need the poetry display more complicated imagery. In the nineteenth century, however, the theme alters in content, or seems to, though perhaps it is rather that a single string of the instrument is touched at any one time, and the others murmur only very faintly. At all events the myth splits up into its component parts. It ceases in the main to be poetry of praise or adoration; and the note of reproach, of fear of falling away, becomes dominant. In remaining public it becomes hortatory, and so becomes different in tone and rhythm. In one point only does it follow the old Augustan pattern, and that is in its insistence on freedom as an absolute value. This is after all a basic life-impulse, common to Caliban and Ariel, and to Sterne's starling. We may not be able to define it; we may engage in difficult distinctions between freedom and liberty; but everybody knows, the man of 'large, sound, round-about sense' in Locke's phrase, knows what the feeling of freedom is. It is immensely important to the poet, being, as Signor Vivante insists, 'a value of *potency* . . unpredictable, opposing sheer conditionality, [it is] a fundamental factor in history'.[1] However sadly we may look at its shrinkage to-day, however much the fear of freedom may exist, however despairingly Mr Alex Comfort may find himself urged to warn his son:

Remember, when you hear them beginning to say Freedom
Look carefully—see who it is they want you to butcher[2]

it remains essential for poets, for without it their creative
energy is shackled, the plastic imagination stifled.

The idea obtruded itself very much, even the lesser poets
leaning heavily on it. You meet it again and again in
Bailey's inflated fustian-Faustian, but universally popular poem: for example, when moralising about stern self-
rule he declares of England that

> To science, learning, law, religion, she
> Adds nature's grace supreme, of liberty.[3]

The note comes out strongly and constantly in Tennyson.
When asked why he was content to subsist in a climate
where he felt ill at ease, depressed by fogs and grey waters,
he unhesitatingly answered that he endured the dismal
conditions because England was the land 'that sober-
suited Freedom chose' (he was here echoing both Thomson and Cowper), and where—somewhat incongruously
if we keep the imagery of the poem in mind—

> Freedom slowly broadens down
> From precedent to precedent.

And if the opposite process seems to be going on now, we
do not find poets celebrating the fact.

Serious patriotic poetry tends to grow more and more
moralistic. It is not only reproachful, as it was with Cowper attacking effeminate individuals, it takes on a warning
note, as seeing the moral dangers ensuing upon national
greatness. Wordsworth wove it in with the theme of
freedom, which had come to England, not as 'nature's
grace supreme', but as something intellectually conceived,
fought for, and won. He was not interested in personifi-
cations, or the flittings of a goddess from abode to abode.
He reached back to tradition, as in the Milton sonnet. All
through the period 1802–03 he was continually haunted by,
as he phrased it, 'some fears un-named', or 'unfilial fears',

K

fears of the failure of the idea; and again and again the depth of this emotion moved him to sonnets which are among those most universally responded to.

> It is not to be thought of that the Flood
> Of British freedom, which to the open Sea
> Of the world's praise from dark antiquity
> Hath flowed with pomp of waters, unwithstood:

and in the conclusion he intertwined at least three themes, unifying the whole with a concentration for him unusual:

> We must be free or die, who speak the tongue
> That Shakespeare spake; the faith and morals hold
> Which Milton held. In every thing we are sprung
> Of Earth's first blood, have titles manifold.

The whole sonnet, indeed, which no one can complain of for not being dense enough, is the compacting of many themes of the myth. It goes on to refer to 'bearing out freights of worth to foreign lands'; in the mention of the 'most famous stream' it picks up the Thames symbol, to which it adds the imagery of knightly armour. All through those years Wordsworth returned to the theme, sometimes even a little incoherently, imploring England to wean its heart from emasculating food, veering from deep depression to what amounts to a jingoistic vaunting of the men of Kent, often in the manner of the schoolboy outbursts of Drayton. For Wordsworth at least the theme of patriotism was poietic, engendering, sometimes, complex and splendid utterance which the general reader remembers and quotes.

And if his greatest verse on this theme is of the reproachful, warning variety, so it was with Swinburne. I mean, of course, his earlier verse, not the later distasteful cock-crowings induced in him by the Boer War. *Songs Before Sunrise* is threaded with the theme; he warns in 'A Watch in the Night', he upbraids in 'An Appeal', where he echoes Croxall's vision of England as an asylum.

It is in his most vigorous onrushing manner, as though
he were intent to exhaust himself rather than the theme:

> Strangers came gladly to thee,
> Exiles, chosen of men,
> Safe for thy sake in thy shade,
> Sat down at thy feet and were free.
> So men spake of thee then;
> Now shall their speaking be stayed?
> Ah, so let it not be!

The complex stanzas though controlled roll on tumul-
tuously: here is the twelfth:

> Be not as tyrant or slave,
> England; be not as these,
> Thou that were other than they.
> Stretch out thine hand but to save;
> Put forth thy strength, and release;
> Lest there arise, if thou slay,
> Thy shame, as a ghost from the grave.

Swinburne is not a poet much to the modern taste; he
seems to be aroused too readily by anything which moves
him, and to fly up with a great clatter of wings. The
Victorians, we know, were nothing if not verbose, volu-
minous, all-inclusive: but even Swinburne, when dis-
mayed at what he thinks a betrayal of the idea can be comparatively concentrated, appealing back to tradition. So in
'Perinde ac Cadaver'—the very title, 'just like a corpse',
is bitter enough—he gives us:

> Cromwell's mother, O breast
> That suckled Milton! thy name
> That was beautiful then, that was blest
> Is it wholly discrowned and deprest,
> Trodden under by sloth into shame?

The vagueness of the fleeting imagery does not obscure
the challenge he is sending out. He was thinking, naturally, in terms of his time, of such as Mazzini. The poem
is no mere vapouring: it has actuality behind it.

A poet, we suppose, will take up a theme, however public it may be, only if he can weld it with his general sense of things, with his philosophy. It was certainly so with Meredith. He especially was always alert to the manhood of Englishmen, as he makes abundantly plain in his novels and letters; and there, as in his poetry, he was always urging a greater liveliness of intellect to overcome a gross, blinding self-satisfaction. Writing in 1891 a poem which seems to us prematurely prophetic with its title 'England, Before the Storm', he rang out:

> Asleep upon her ancient deeds,
> She hugs the vision plethora breeds,
> And counts her manifold increase
> Of treasure in the fruits of peace . . .

and so on, to proceed to the next stanza, where the scorn sharpens, to an idea more specifically Meredithian:

> She, impious to the Lord of Hosts,
> The valour of her offspring boasts,
> Mindless that now on land and main
> His heeded prayer is active brain.
> No more great heart may guard the home,
> Save eyed and armed and skilled to cleave
> Yon swallower wave with shroud of foam
> We see not distant heave.

The imagery is extraordinarily confused—nobody can accuse that of being mere poetry of statement—but it is clear what he is getting at. Mind must issue out of mud; the 'active brain' must supplement mere animal courage. He is deeply moved. The old classical analogy (the state compared with the body, an intellectual concept) gives way to the sea-imagery that with him is always the sign of emotion, involving something of deep significance. But I will return for the moment to the phrase 'impious to the Lord of Hosts' which at once brings to mind Kipling's 'Recessional' with its refrain:

Lord God of Hosts, be with us yet,
Lest we forget, lest we forget.

It is one of the ironies of literary history that Kipling
should be almost universally regarded as a jingo poet,
whereas he is for ever moralising, warning, reproaching
England for the stain on her garment's hem. His vision of
the Empire was, as Mr Eliot says, 'almost that of an
empire laid up in heaven', and he is the last of our poets
to attempt to integrate the Great Myth, notably in the
small collection called 'A Song of the English'. There are
notes here and there, as in the line

Swift shuttles of an Empire's loom that weaves us main to main:

but the mystique comes out in 'The Song of the Dead':

We were the dreamers, dreaming greatly, in the man-stifled town;
We yearned beyond the sky-line where the strange roads go down.
Came the Whisper, came the Vision, came the Power with the
    Need,
Till the Soul that is not man's soul, was lent to us to lead.

In 'Recessional', however, there begins a curious opposite process which we might call the disintegration of the
myth. It is, to quote Mr Eliot again, 'one of the poems
from which something breaks through from a deeper level
than that of the mind of a conscious observer of political
and social affairs—something which has the true prophetic inspiration'. It may be argued that Kipling, in a
sense, is a poor illustration of my argument that public
themes are such as force themselves involuntarily into a
poet's work, however much they may seem outside his
ordinary run, for much of Kipling's thought is political.
But 'Recessional' is very much to my purpose, since the
idea behind it was coming into common consciousness,
with the sense of imperial responsibility to something outside man, 'the soul that is not man's soul'.

And Meredith takes up the theme, with a last faint echo
of the myth. Some five years after Kipling's poem, in

'The Voyage of the Ophir', he suggests that with the old
veins of England 'toned . . . with streams of youth' from
the Dominions, we shall

> Prove to the world of brows down-bent
> That in the Britain thus endowed,
> Imperial means beneficent,
>   And strength to service vowed.

Then, in 'The Warning', he takes up Kipling's

> If, drunk with sight of power we loose
>   Wild tongues that have not Thee in awe,

and writes:

> Concerns it most ourselves, who with our gas—
> This little Isle's insatiable greed
> For continents—filled to inflation burst.
> So do ripe nations into squalor pass,
> When, driven by herds by their old pirate thirst
> They scorn the brain's wild search for virtuous light.

Again the plethora, the brain, the typical half-imagery. It
embodies the knowledge familiar to the poetic imagination
that, as Mr Wilson Knight puts it, 'All worldly power is
sin-struck at the core'; and this is the point to which the
more complex sense of patriotism—not the intuitive sense
of belonging to the soil—has taken our poets. It is something always uneasily present in the general mind, which
the poet, if he is to be widely read, must, if not express, at
least show an awareness of, as one of the assumptions by
which the average thinking man lives.

Something then, is happening to the myth, with this
increasing complexity and growing general awareness of
the issues involved. It has undergone a subtle change. It
no longer satisfies easily, as we can tell from the confused
imagery which accompanies its statement, except, again,
with Kipling, whose use of Biblical phrase is more notable
here than in most other parts of his work. But even with
Kipling, in some ways closest to it, the myth has lost the

sense of permanence, of being eternal truth, such as must reside in every myth. It is all fleeting:

> Cities and Thrones and Powers
> Stand in Time's eye,
> Almost as long as flowers
> Which daily die,[4]

and the moment will come

> When all our pomp of yesterday
> Is one with Nineveh and Tyre.

He was always insistent that power was only lent, and will be taken away if the trust is betrayed. And it is becoming apparent to men that all empire, however 'beneficent', is fatally flawed; the worship of wealth eats into it, the worship that Tennyson was vocal in railing against. So what seems to be happening is that the myth is dissolving into another myth; it is being sublimated as other themes have been, or at any rate is being enlarged. It is becoming inclusive of the whole world. We find it clearly stated in *Locksley Hall*, in a couplet everybody knows. After the prophetic vision of Armageddon, where Tennyson speaks of 'the nations' airy navies grappling in the central blue', he goes on

> Till the war-drum throbbed no longer, and the battle-flags were furl'd
> In the Parliament of man, the Federation of the world.

But he had no illusions; he wasn't possessed by the brave optimism of a decade or so of our own century which looked upon all this as being just round the corner. It was millenniums ahead, part of a slow organic process of evolution, of the kind Meredith claimed to be in process. He broods over it in a very late poem, 'The Making of Man':

> Where is one that, born of woman, altogether can escape
> From the lower world within him, moods of tiger, or of ape?
> Man as yet is being made, and ere the crowning Age of ages
> Shall not aeon after aeon pass and touch him into shape?

All about him shadow still, but, while races flower and fade,
Prophet eyes may catch the glory slowly gaining in the shade,
Till the peoples all are one, and all their voices blend in choric
Hallelujah to the Maker, 'It is finished, Man is made'.

The idea of the federation of man is not of course even as
new as the imperial form it took in the Great Myth; the
Stoics held the idea of one universal city, and William
Penn, in our own country and era, tried to give it practical form. It is now becoming almost a common assumption.

The natural history of this theme varies from that of the
others; there exist also a number of sub-themes which I
have barely touched upon, the battle-piece and the patriotic
song—but these belong to vulgar rather than to public
poetry. Yet it has after all many points in common; it has
its didactic phases, those where it is absorbed into description; it acquires imagery, and while gathering to itself and
supporting a number of other themes, comes to express
itself symbolically. It then begins to split up, to be transformed, to be merged into something else; or the main
stream, to vary my metaphor, becomes variously chan-
nelled; some themes shrink, others are lost in the sands of the
delta, some persist, to run into the sea of general apprehension. In so far as the sense of kinship with one's fellows goes, the last is what seems to have happened here.
Take Hardy. He is, in some sense, a patriot of the soil,
of the people tied to the soil; the maid and her wight will
go whispering by long after war's annals have faded. As
for patriotism itself, he seems to have accepted it as needful in the great working out of things; at least he did so in
The Dynasts, which is in a sense a patriotic poem, if patriotism can at all emerge from the dark blanket of the
Immanent Will. But it is he who most decisively expresses
the new myth by which we all now largely live, if only in
tremulous hope. In 'Departure', written on seeing men
embark for war, he asks, how long it shall be before patriotism

> . . . grown Godlike, scorns to stand
> Bondslave to realms, but circle earth and seas?

and we hear the reaching forward again in 'His Country':

> I traced the whole terrestrial round,
>   Homing the other side;
> Then said I, 'What is there to bound
>   My denizenship?' It seems that I have found
>   Its scope to be world-wide—

But the theme, one would think, at least in this aspect of it, has passed out of the realm of intuitive apprehension. It has progressively fallen into the clutches of the politicians, where the formative imagination is restricted by administrative yearnings and wranglings at conferences. The poet has nothing to do there. He can only hope that his own sense can seep in through some unnoticed chink in the heavily baized doors.

But let us see where patriotism in its simpler connotation stands to-day. If once it could inspire poets to great utterance, it was because it could create a myth. Now the whole deep sense of it is shot with uneasiness. It is as though it nagged at the poets' subconscious, as something suppressed, though not yet *re*pressed so as to appear disguised in symbolic forms. It will out, even against the grain, as it did with Mr Charles Madge in the decade when poetry was largely directed by intellectual Marxism motivated by a humane rage against social conditions. In a poem in which he vociferates 'Lenin, thou should'st be living at this hour, England hath need of thee'—a wry grimace, an outraging gesture—he breaks out:

> Yes, England, I was at school with you, I've known
> Your hills come open to me, calling me crying
> With a bird voice, and passing I have been haunted
> By a wood, I have loved you, slept with you
> By moonlight. Walking home by fields known
> I have seen the prints of those feet, being alone
> Found you, talked to you, for you my laughing and crying
> Have been no secret, you have known when I was lying.

You are always beside me, so I go haunted.
You are my one believed-in ghost. I've vaunted
And venerated you, England, knowing you
'D rise from the dead and prove my superstition true.[5]

That, in spite of the repetition of the words 'crying', 'haunted', 'known', is more than a cry of despair. It voices an inescapable faith; it is a new form of the mystique, though what it embodies is left unstated. The one believed-in ghost is compounded of place and people and tradition, of ideals that change their form but not their purpose. And in spite of what seems to be a common detachment of poets from public themes, patriotism spasmodically recurs, as though it were something deep in the self that will not be denied, whatever of Martin Decoud a man may include in his intellectual flirtations. Thus, Mr John Wain offered to 'New Soundings' what he entitled 'Patriotic Poem' on

This mildewed island
Rained on and beaten flat by bombs and water . . .

which concludes

Yet from the cauldron
Where her hard bones are formed by time and anguish
Rises the living breath of all her children;
And her deep heart and theirs who can distinguish.[6]

It is sad and timorous; nevertheless it expresses a chastened, historical consciousness, supported by a faith in the living breath of the people, able to wrench triumph from decline, and maintain its own ethos whatever may come. The emotional pressure was great enough to produce poetry. Patriotism may yet serve as a public theme, though it does not seem coherent enough. But it has at least returned to one of its old elements, the sense of local community.

THE BROKEN CISTERN

I HAVE tried to trace the natural history of three public themes: and perhaps what is most significant to me about them is that they chose themselves. They cropped up, almost everywhere, in great and minor poets alike, undergoing changes, being merged into something else, carrying superstructures, but persisting for some centuries. Though they varied in response both to the intuitions of the poets and to the sense of the age in which these lived, they were always to hand as at least underlying themes.

How does all this link up with the questions I asked myself at the beginning? Can any definite answers be suggested? What are the reasons why poetry is no longer generally read? Are we in Goethe's fourth age, that of chaos, the furthest removed from the one where poetry is possible? Was Peacock justified in saying that man has outgrown poetry? If these were right, then all discussions of poetry are meaningless. Yet I for one pin my faith to the doctrine that for a satisfactory civilisation to exist, imaginative writing must be widely read, noting the accepted fact that poetry is the most highly-geared and inclusive form of such writing; but adding that to be nourishing it must respond to and express general states of being. More, it must inform them, give them meaning, since this is the function of the poetic intuition, all the more important to-day, because there is nothing else that will produce any kind of universalisation leading to that kind of generally shared state of being without which no civilisation is possible.

'What!' I shall be asked, in an incredulous even scan-

dalised tone, 'Do you want poetry to be elevating?' At
least I want it to be releasing, illuminating, reconciling,
and to deal with the things that most matter to most men.
Elevating? That's as the human situation may resolve itself. Poetry may merely ask the question:

> . . . what rough beast, its hour come round at last,
> Slouches toward Bethlehem to be born?[1]

Or it may help to determine some general basis for living
which exists as a rule only vaguely in the hearts of most
men. For the poet is not merely a passive transmitter, a
gramophone record. He is willy-nilly a prophet and seer
as well. And he must give delight, the deep delight that
comes from a realisation of as much of the complete being
as is possible or relevant at any one moment, in a song of
Campion's or an invocation in *Paradise Lost*. Moreover
the poets are, or have been, the preservers, the trans-
mitters, of our profoundest culture—and by culture I do
not mean the collection of old furniture or new pictures
nor even pious ejaculations such as *soyez bons pour les
animaux*, but the great body of largely subconscious assumptions by which most of us live. In the absence of any
general adherence to the doctrines of formal religion, or
accepted view of the way the universe works and of our
moral adjustment to it, who but the poets can be the vital
energisers of tradition, the sort of tradition which lies at
the back of most men's minds and actions?

But at the present day poetry is not generally read in
the way that it used to be, and surely this is partly because
it does not offer people what they want to read about; it
does not illumine the assumptions by which they live.
The excuse may be made that it reflects our present,
incoherent, uneasy state, one in which we seem to have no
direction; and the poets, it can be argued, feel that there
is no 'large general state of mind' which they are bound to
meet, and of which they will want to give their version.
As Yeats put it:

Shakespearean fish swam the sea, far away from land;
Romantic fish swam in nets coming to the hand;
What are all those fish that lie gasping on the strand?[2]

I doubt whether that is necessarily decisive. We have
heard before of 'This strange disease of modern life,
With its sick hurry, its divided aims'. Yet though we do
not lack extremely able poets, vital, exploratory, sensitive
to words, they seem to limit themselves voluntarily to
recording fleeting experiences, to writing footnotes on ideas,
to embodying fugitive thoughts, sometimes piercing
enough, but isolated. The hoped-for general reader may
well ask 'What *are* all these fish that lie gasping on the
strand?' That seems specially true of the younger genera-
tion, which may be one searching for itself. It does not apply
to a few of the older poets, Mr Eliot, Miss Sitwell, Mr
Muir, and one or two others, who well know what they
would be at, but tend to express rather too special philosophies of their own. They speak, however miraculously,
to the few: and employing as they do their own symbolic,
but not necessarily private language, the barrier between
them and the general reader is formidable.

Perhaps the very attempt to universalise is to-day a
delusion and a dangerous snare; William James, indeed,
called it 'a bit of perverse sentimentalism'. Certainly Mr
Muir seems to be stating a truth when he says:

The more a writer tries to render his vision of the world in its
completeness, the more irrevocably he turns it into his private
world. The more carefully he connects everything with everything, the less is his reader able to connect anything with
anything.[3]

But to argue that poetry has to abandon its old bardic
function and be written only for a trained audience, would
be a conclusion almost as deadly as Peacock's, for it
implies that the poet is to explore only the world within,
ignoring that without, making no attempt to relate the
two. No fructifying influence would be felt. Or it might

imply that in our present state of fragmentation there must be two kinds of poetry, one, such as Dr Leavis thinks alone will persist, written for the elect who 'understand' poetry, the poet using a very specialised idiom for imparting his intuitions of reality; and another kind written for the sensitive intelligent general readers who want to have affirmed, or widened, the intuitions they share in common. Also a dreary prospect. The situation is indeed menacing. As Mr Wyndham Lewis has lately written:

> The only people who understand about science are scientists . . . the difference between a good painting and a bad painting is only known, in the last analysis, to painters . . .

and so on to include poetry and poets. He proceeds:

> The quality of a work of art is very difficult to assess. It requires a great deal of experience to be able to do so. In times when a sizeable population . . . had much leisure, a certain number—in addition to those that wrote themselves—reached the point where they could tell a good book when they saw one. But at the present day, apart from universities, where could we find anyone competent to evaluate a work of literature?[4]

Very flattering, no doubt, for universities, and, alas! largely true: but if poetry is to be written exclusively for university dons, it is hardly a healthy state of affairs. Are they to be the sole arbiters? Heaven forbid! For how can a specialised little group, 'evaluating' qualities which, however exciting to themselves, can have no meaning for a 'sizeable population', decide what will delight, will nourish, the reasonable reader Dryden appealed to? The voice of the benevolent despot booms from the eighteenth century:

> By the common sense of readers uncorrupted with literary prejudices, after all the refinements of subtilty and the dogmatism of learning, must be finally decided all claim to poetical honours.[5]

Yet the situation may not be as dismal as all this implies. Mr J. W. Saunders wrote not long ago:

The audience a poet *wants* and the audience he knows he will *get* are seldom identical. Usually he has to look two ways, keeping one eye on the chosen few who will understand his aspirations, and the other on the general public who will not, but who will nevertheless demand their moneysworth.[6]

Their moneysworth of what? That is the present question. Housman was convinced that:

Most readers, when they think that they are admiring poetry are deceived by their inability to analyse their sensations . . . they are really admiring not the poetry of the passage before them, but something else in it which they like better than the poetry.[7]

The something else, I suggest, is as often as not a public theme such as I have been discussing; if there is any validity in my natural history of these themes, it would seem that they were very much present when poetry was widely read. My contention is then that the poet can get his two audiences by merging a public theme with the explorations of the reality it is his prime need to undertake.

The latter certainly it is essential for him to do. As Professor Day Lewis has said of himself and his fellow poets, 'We do not write to be understood; we write to understand.' That we accept; but here is a real crux: for as Mr C. S. Lewis has written:

It may well be that the author who claims to write neither for patron nor public but for himself has done our art an incalculable harm . . . by teaching us to emphasise the public's duty of 'recognition' instead of the artist's duty to teach and delight.[8]

Professor Day Lewis, however, provides a loophole by quoting from Mr Owen Barfield, 'To *start* from a personal experience does not necessarily mean to finish with one', as we have seen perhaps with Emily Brontë. And after all, for the poet to write that he may understand does not necessarily mean that he doesn't *want* to be understood. No doubt at first by his fellow poets, who will see what he is after, and be able to 'place' his work, taste its quality.

But he would not be human if he did not want more, as is made clear from the way that poets assault the theatre. There may be some who, like Landor, do not mind if they dine late, and are content if the table is well-lighted, and the guests few and select; he has got what he wished for (it's a pity the guests should be so sparse): but more are like Elizabeth Barrett Browning who wanted her poetry to 'rush into the drawing-rooms, and the like, meeting face to face the humanity of the age'. A more convincing witness is Shelley, who wrote to John Gisborne:

> It is impossible to compose except under the strong excitement of an assurance of finding sympathy in what you write. . . . Lord Byron is in this respect fortunate. He touched the chord to which a million hearts responded. . . .

Byron embraced a number of public themes; but so did Shelley. Thus it may occur to us to ask why it was that Byron reached the million hearts, and Shelley was tortured by the poor reception his work met with. He himself gives the answer: for he goes on to say about Byron:

> He touched the chord to which a million hearts responded, and the coarse music which he produced to please them, disciplined him to the perfection to which he now approaches.[9]

So now another question asks itself.

Is there anything which distinguishes public poetry, such as Milton or Pope or Wordsworth wrote, and which has become ingrained in our consciousness, and makes it differ from that which deals with the private emotions? Not that everybody does not feel these to a greater or less poignant degree, but they belong to the realm of private things. The poetry I have been concerned with is popular, not in the sense that it springs from the people, but that in dealing with common themes it binds the general readers together. Is it then differently written? For it may be that the poetry which develops a public theme has to be patently musical, strongly rhythmed, and—this is

perhaps the important point—free of recondite symbol
which it needs the schools to elucidate. It tends, I suggest,
to be tranquil—at least in the very great poets; it is pellu-
cid, lacking normally the complex density or the dialectic
teasing which satisfies contemporary academic demands.
It has to be expressed in such terms as make the intuitions
readily apprehended, in phrases that are portable, easily
remembered and muttered to one's self. Thus 'metaphysical tension' would impair it; nor is there any call for
'wit' in the sense in which the 'Schools' have come to use
the word. Naturally it varies, not only from poet to poet,
but according to the state of development of the themes
themselves, as they come to carry more or less superstructure. Yet since all are intended to cause men to fit
into the scheme of things, they belong to Collingwood's
category of 'magic' poetry. This acts, not so much on
the intellect, as on the nerves. Its chief impact is, as Mr
Lawrence Durrell tells us—other poets have phrased it
more urbanely—on the guts.[10] Since it inculcates, however little it may mean to, an attitude to existence, since it
wants to convey an impression to be shared, it tends to be
incantatory, whether the theme is moralistic as Stoicism is,
or whether, like scientism, it calls for intellectual adjustment, or, like patriotism, utters an emotional call.

With science it seems to involve more imagery, as one
would expect where a new reality is to be explored. True,
anything new can be explained didactically in plain
plodding verse; but it can be imaginatively seized by the
reader—and perhaps by the poet himself—only in terms
of something else, that is, by metaphor. But for poetry to
be widely read the metaphor has to relate to the familiar;
in making the unlike like, one of the terms has to be well-
known, though metaphor can have meaning only if fused
with the sense of the unity of existence by the heat of the
poet's imagination. Thus little of the poetry I have quoted
provides recondite illumination; Shelley might rank a
good deal of it as coarse. Yet it answers the most common

L

needs of humanity, whence its enormous importance. After all, as Coleridge said, all poetry need not have the highest relish, and every one of us would join him in abhorring the idea of an Act of Uniformity being passed upon poets. If sometimes the poet begins, like Byron, by uttering coarse music, the reader himself necessarily begins with the obvious, responding to verse of little subtlety, imagery that is simple. 'Unpoetical natures', as J. S. Mill said, 'are precisely those which require poetic cultivation.' To-day an Act of Uniformity is being imposed upon them also—and they evade poetry.

How indeed are a million hearts to respond? We* in universities, of course, are very properly eager to discover the pure 'poetic' qualities; but ought we not, in the interests of poetry itself, to subject to critical attention the 'something else in it' that Housman mentioned, so that the poetry may be ordinarily read? You may say that we are not responsible. But can we evade the responsibility? Why, after all do we write? That we may influence; and members of the general public do sometimes read what we say. And if the common means of transmission, shall I call it, is the reviewer, he himself is largely moulded by what the universities talk about. And the question I ask myself is whether the dwindled popular appeal of poetry may not be partly our fault. In paying as we do such attention to matters which only the specialist can be at home with, haven't we, with great ceremony, brought poetry, not into the wide halls of judgment, but into the academic laboratory? I call to mind what Shaftesbury said about philosophy in his day:

> She is no longer *active* in the World; nor can hardly, with any advantage, be brought upon the publick *Stage*. We have immured her [poor Lady!] in Colleges and Cells; and have set her servilely to such Works as those in the Mines. . . . The School-syllogism, and the *Elixir* are the choicest of her products.[11]

---

* I must apologetically remind the reader here that these lectures were originally delivered by a don to a university audience.

I will not maliciously press the possible parallel; for whatever may be said about the New Criticism, its forebears
and relations, I for one am immensely grateful for their
labours. And after all, every critic must pursue what most
enthralls him: every don to his his bone. But should this
highly intellectual, erudite pursuit be our only interest?
Ought we not to 'evaluate' in a different way the kind of
poetry such as Mill found in Wordsworth, from which
men seem to 'draw from a source of inward joy, of sympathetic and imaginative pleasure, which could be shared
in by all human beings'? Have we not forsaken the fountain of living waters, and made ourselves cisterns, broken
cisterns, that can hold no water?

I am, as I said at the outset, pleading for a simpler
approach. I would wish us to relate our poetry to the
common feeling of the day, as well as formulating density,
ambiguity, dialectic, and so on. Isn't it still true, as Keats
said, that 'Poetry should be great and unobtrusive, a thing
which enters into one's soul, and does not startle or amaze
with itself, but with its subject'?[12] For though you cannot
tell a poet what he should write about, nor how he should
write, you may be able to create a climate of criticism
which he might wish to enter. If the poet's readers are to be
found only among highly trained specialists, it is for them
he will write: he knows they will understand. Naturally if
you think that the immuring of poetry in colleges and
cells doesn't matter, well and good. But if you believe, as
I do, that there is in man a deep need for the sort of statement that poetry makes, and that civilisation can in part
be shaped by the satisfaction of this need, then the bring-
ing into being of a different climate of appreciation
is of supreme importance. It is only too certain that a
small critical tribunal can silently exercise a lethal censor-
ship.

Finally, I would say that whatever the state of affairs
may be, the constant recurrence of such themes as I have
been treating of is significant, even vital, since it would

seem that only through such has poetry, with its illumination of common assumptions, become part of the everyday spiritual nourishment of the general reader. Great
poets have acknowledged them, transformed them, made
them habitual; and it might be argued that they were
great poets precisely because they did so. By writing
poetry relative to these themes they became part of the
national consciousness: it was poetry 'distilled Through
all the needful uses of our lives'. Or put it this way: the
public themes served as conductors of what the trained
readers think more important in poetry: they made possible the transformation of the commonplace attitude into
something more vividly, more creatively, apprehended,
enabling the poet *then*, but not before, to break in with
his new light, his intense personal vision. And these very
themes, transmuted to meet present-day needs and apprehensions of life, might well serve again. For do human
beings in reality vary much throughout the centuries?
Do we not, in our passion to understand the past (or in
our natural pride in being exclusive specialists), tend to
exaggerate the differences rather too much? It is doubtful
whether in historical times men have been endowed with
different modes of apprehension. As Schopenhauer put it,
we have always before us

> merely the one creature, *essentially* identical and unchangeable,
> busying itself with the very same things to-day, and yesterday,
> and forever. . . . This identity, preserved through all changes, is
> founded on the fundamental qualities of human hearts and brains.[13]

The idiom varies, the immediate object of attention shifts:
but it would appear that whenever men go outside their
conflicts with God, or their personal emotions, or the
investigation of their hearts, certain common underlying
currents of being emerge—the sense of the oneness of
humanity, of its place in the universe, or the love of the
country which bred them. They fall back upon 'the common sense of what men were and are', to use Marston's

phrase. It is when poets fail to do so that they lose touch with the public that looks to them for justification of their own responsible selves, for illumination of the assumptions by which, consciously or not, they live, act, and in the fullest sense have their being.

REFERENCES

INTRODUCTION AND CHAPTER I.

1 *Nones.* 'Under which Lyre'.
2 *The Personal Heresy*, pp. 138–9.
3 *The Derelict Day*. 'Troopship'.
4 *Twenty-five Poems*. 'To a Conscript of 1940'.
5 Sir John Davies. *Nosce Teipsum* St. 260 *seq.*
6 *Selected Essays*. 'Shakespeare and the Stoicism of Seneca'.
7 *Language as Gesture*, p. 259.
8 *The Excursion*, Book IV. 324 *seq.* See also Selincourt's edition, Vol. V, p. 424.
9 E.g. Seneca, *The Happy Life*, L'Estrange. Ep. 126. Or Marcus Aurelius, *Meditations*, end of Book II. Trs. Collier.
10 Act IV. Sc.i.
11 Book IV. xxix. Trs. Collier.
12 Act III. Sc. i.
13 *The Scourge of Villany*. 'To Detraction'.
14 Ep. 93. Trs. L'Estrange.
15 *Collected Poems 1929–36*. 'Transitional Poem 23'.

CHAPTER II.

1 An account of the author, prefixed to the *Poems on Several Occasions* by Stephen Duck, 1736.
2 *Essay on Man*, Ep. II. 101.
3 *Ibid*, Ep. IV. 29.
4 End of the first chapter.
5 *Essay on Man*, Ep. I. 289.
6 *Meditations*, II. ii. Trs. Collier.
7 *Ibid*, V. iii.
8 *The Classical Influence in English Literature*, p. 411.
9 *Discourses*, I. 6. Trs. Matheson. Loeb Classics.
10 *Ibid*, I. 18.
11 *Cogitations*, VIII. 9. Trs. Davidson. Loeb Classics.
12 *Ash Wednesday*, I.
13 *Songs Before Sunrise*. 'Prelude'.
14 See *Evolution and Ethics; passim.*
15 *A Shropshire Lad*, XLV.
16 *The Dynasts*, I. V. iv and II. II. iii.
17 *No More Ghosts*. 'Certain Mercies'.
18 *Collected Poems*, 1952.

[19] Prize-winning entry in Festival of Britain competition. Penguin *Poems* 1951.
[20] *Nones*. 'A Walk after Dark'.
[21] *Elegies for the Dead in Cyrenaica*.
[22] 'The Listener'. 26 June 1952.

CHAPTER III.
[1] 'Ode to the Memory of Sir Isaac Newton'.
[2] *Defence of Poetry*.
[3] Preface to *Lyrical Ballads*.
[4] *Don Juan*, X. i.
[5] *Letters from Iceland* (with Louis MacNeice) 'Letter to Lord Byron', Part III.
[6] *For the Time Being*. 'Choral Fugue'.
[7] Post-script to 'Notes and Observations on *The Empress of Morocco*.'
[8] *Lives of the Poets*. Dryden. Ed. Hill.
[9] *Loves of the Plants*. Interlude I.
[10] Shakespeare, *Troilus and Cressida*, III. iii. 109. I owe this quotation in the present context to Dr I. A. Richards.
[11] *Science and English Poetry*, p. 164. Mr Heard's book is *The Third Morality*.
[12] *Archetypal Patterns in Poetry*, p. 323.
[13] 'Yale Review', Vol. XXXIX, No. I, Autumn 1949. 'Emotive Language Still'.
[14] *The Life of Reason*, p. 172.
[15] *Concerning the Nature of Things*.
[16] *Science and Poetry*, p. 51.
[17] *Collected Poems*.
[18] 'Nine' No. VIII. Spring 1952.
[19] *Devine Weekes and Workes*, I. 3. 174.
[20] *The Man in the Moone*, 369 *seq*.
[21] 'On Poetry: a Rapsody', 337 *seq*.
[22] T. S. Eliot. 'The Love Song of Alfred J. Prufrock'.
[23] Advertisement to *The Economy of Nature*.
[24] *The Loves of the Plants*. Canto I. 117 *seq*. Previous quotations Canto IV. 2. 34, and Interlude II.
[25] *A Hope for Poetry*, Ch. IX.
[26] *Collected Poems 1929–36*.
[27] *The Still Centre*.
[28] *The Economy of Vegetation*. Canto I. 289 *seq*.
[29] *The Galloping Centaur*. 'A Ride in a Sports Car.'

CHAPTER IV.
[1] *The Origins of Science*, p. 1.
[2] *The Dream of Learning; passim*.
[3] Quoted in *Augustan Satire*, by Ian Jack.
[4] 'Poem on Sir Isaac Newton', 11 *seq*.

[5] 'To the Memory of Sir Isaac Newton', 82 *seq.*
[6] *Newton Demands the Muse.*
[7] *The Excursion*, II. 188 *seq.*
[8] *The Daemon of the World*, Part I. 241 *seq.*
[9] *Pleasures of the Imagination.* 1744 version, II. 126 *seq.*
[10] *Science and the Modern World*, Chapter III. English ed. p. 69.
[11] *A Newton among Poets*, p. 164. See also his *The Magic Plant.*
[12] *Prometheus Unbound*, IV. 238 *seq.*
[13] *The Book of Los*, IV.
[14] *The Magic Plant*, p. 281.
[15] *Prometheus Unbound*, V. 238 *seq.*
[16] *Defence of Poetry.*
[17] 'To Mr Congreve', ll. 93, 94.
[18] *Creation*, Book II.
[19] *Essay on Man*, Ep. II. 35
[20] *The Dunciad*, Book IV. 465 *seq.*
[21] *The Prelude*, 1850, Book II. 210 *seq.*
[22] Letter to Thomas Butts. 22 November, 1802. Nonesuch ed. p. 1068.
[23] See generally *The Road to Xanadu.*
[24] 21 October, 1801.
[25] *In Memoriam*, cxxiii.
[26] *In Memoriam*, lv and lvi.
[27] *The Dry Salvages*, Section III.
[28] *The Excursion*, Book III. Extracts from 161–89.
[29] *Collected Poems* 1925–48. 'The Kingdom', Section VI.
[30] *A Correct Compassion*. Title poem.
[31] Published in 'Public Opinion'.

CHAPTER V.

[1] *New Country.* 'Hymn'.
[2] *Timber; or Discoveries*, Vol VI
[3] *Autobiographies*, p. 235.
[4] 'Sussex'. Definitive edition of *Verse* 1940, p. 213.
[5] *Character of a Trimmer.*
[6] *Areopagitica.*
[7] *New Country.* 'Me, March, you do with your movements . . .'
[8] *Last Poems.* 'Under Ben Bulben'.
[9] *The Task*, Book II. 'The Time-Piece', 206 *seq.*
[10] *Devine Weekes and Workes*, I. 2, 899 *seq.*
[11] *Ibid.*
[12] 'The Jacobite's Lament'.
[13] Collected Poems.
[14] *Ardours and Endurances.* 'At the Wars'.
[15] *Severn and Somme.* 'Strange Service'.
[16] *England Under the Stuarts.*
[17] *The Theme of Patriotism in the Poetry of the Early Eighteenth Century.*
Proceedings of the British Academy. Vol. XXXV.

[18] *The Fleece*, Book IV. 661 *seq.*
[19] *Maxims Concerning Patriotism*, No. 2. Ed. A. C. Fraser, III. p. 455.
[20] *The Winding Stair*, Vol. II. 'Blood and the Moon'.

CHAPTER VI.

[1] *English Poetry*, p. 239, under Tennyson. The importance of the idea of freedom to English poets comes out *passim* in this book.
[2] *The Signal to Engage*. 'The Song of Lazarus', VI.
[3] *Festus* 1889 ed. (50th Anniversary!) p. 151.
[4] *Puck of Pook's Hill*. 'A Centurion of the Thirtieth'.
[5] *New Country*. 'Letter to the Intelligentsia'.
[6] 'The Listener' 12 June 1952.

CONCLUSION.

[1] Yeats. *Michael Roberts and the Dancer*. 'The Second Coming'.
[2] Yeats. *The Winding Stair*. 'Three Movements'.
[3] Review 'Correspondences', *The Observer*, 2 November 1952.
[4] *The Writer and the Absolute*, p. 34.
[5] Samuel Johnson. *Lives of the Poets*. Ed. Hill, III. 441.
[6] 'The Façade of Morality'. 'Journal of English Literary History', Vol. 19, No. 2, p. 81. June 1952.
[7] *The Name and Nature of Poetry*.
[8] *Oxford History of English Literature*, Vol. III, p. 529.
[9] 18 July, 1822. *Letters*, ed. Ingpen, II. 977.
[10] See generally his *A Key to Modern Poetry*.
[11] *Characteristics*. 'Miscellaneous Reflections', I. 3.
[12] Letter to Reynolds. 3 February 1818.
[13] Quoted by Erich Heller in *The Disinherited Mind*, p. 60.

INDEX

This is meant as a working index, and names, not very significant in the present context and mentioned only once, are not included. The numerals in italics indicate that the author mentioned is being quoted.

Dates have not been given of authors who are still living, or who may be considered as near-contemporaries.

155